Why Manners Matter

ALSO BY LUCINDA HOLDFORTH

True Pleasures:
A Memoir of Women in Paris

Why Manners Matter

The Case for Civilized Behavior
in a Barbarous World

Lucinda Holdforth

AMY EINHORN BOOKS

Published by G. P. Putnam's Sons
a member of Penguin Group (USA) Inc.
New York

AMY EINHORN BOOKS
Published by G. P. Putnam's Sons
Publishers Since 1838
Published by the Penguin Group
Penguin Group (USA) Inc., 375 Hudson Street, New York, New York 10014,
USA • Penguin Group (Canada), 90 Eglinton Avenue East, Suite 700, Toronto, Ontario
M4P 2Y3, Canada (a division of Pearson Canada Inc.) • Penguin Books Ltd,
80 Strand, London WC2R 0RL, England • Penguin Ireland, 25 St Stephen's Green,
Dublin 2, Ireland (a division of Penguin Books Ltd) • Penguin Group (Australia),
250 Camberwell Road, Camberwell, Victoria 3124, Australia (a division of Pearson Australia
Group Pty Ltd) • Penguin Books India Pvt Ltd, 11 Community Centre, Panchsheel Park,
New Delhi–110 017, India • Penguin Group (NZ), 67 Apollo Drive, Rosedale,
North Shore 0632, New Zealand (a division of Pearson New Zealand Ltd) • Penguin Books
(South Africa) (Pty) Ltd, 24 Sturdee Avenue, Rosebank, Johannesburg 2196, South Africa

Penguin Books Ltd, Registered Offices:
80 Strand, London WC2R 0RL, England

Library of Congress Cataloging-in-Publication Data

Holdforth, Lucinda, date.
Why manners matter : the case for civilized behavior in a barbarous world / Lucinda Holdforth.
p. cm.
ISBN 978-0-399-15532-1
1. Etiquette. I. Title.
BJ1853.H67 2009 2008026142
395—dc22

Printed in the United States of America
1 3 5 7 9 10 8 6 4 2

BOOK DESIGN BY MICHELLE MCMILIAN

To Syd Hickman

CONTENTS

Introduction   *1*

I. Because man is an animal   7
   . . . a social one   13
   . . . with a habitat to protect   18

2. Because manners are more important than laws   23
   . . . less invasive than morals   31
   . . . and better than social confusion   35

3. Because manners nurture our equality   45
   . . . modify self-esteem   54
   . . . and connect the self to society   65

4. Because sovereignty demands self-sovereignty   73
   . . . order is necessary to freedom   83
   . . . and manners reconcile liberty to stability   89

5. Because who else can we call on?   93
   . . . rudeness won't make us authentic   97
   . . . manners aren't just the tool of right-wing bigots   102
   . . . and they advance social progress   112

6. Because McDonald's doesn't own manners   121
   . . . corporations don't own our souls   128
   . . . and manners are no barrier to greatness   138

7. Because manners give us dignity   145
   . . . improve communication   152
   . . . prevent premature intimacy   157
   . . . unlock our humanity   162
   . . . and make life beautiful   166

Afterword   169
Further Reading   173
Acknowledgments   175

*Zilu asked what makes a gentleman. The Master said: Through
self-cultivation, he achieves dignity.*

Is that all?

Through self-cultivation he spreads his peace to his neighbours.

Is that all?

Through self-cultivation he spreads his peace to all the people.

*Through self-cultivation to spread one's peace to all the people:
even Yao and Shun could not have aimed for more.*

—CONFUCIUS, *The Analects*

(from the translation by Simon Leys, 1997)

Why Manners Matter

INTRODUCTION

Perhaps it's wise to begin with a disclaimer.

When I told my mother that I was writing an essay on the subject of manners, I heard a long and intense silence down the phone followed by, "You. *You?* We sent you to that expensive school and all you learned was how to swear."

I then rang my friend Rachel, told her my plan and, in anticipation of indignant sympathy, mentioned my mother's dispiriting response. There was another long pause before Rachel's reply: "Well, you do say 'fuck' a lot."

As word got around, friends and acquaintances appeared at my apartment proffering etiquette books. At first I was flattered by their interest, but then it occurred to me that this might be a very polite way indeed to send a message.

This was all rather unnerving.

Arguing the case for manners—when not famous for possessing them—may seem like the literary equivalent of moving into a glass house and setting neat piles of stones outside with a sign inviting passersby to help themselves.

And that's just the start of the challenge.

"Good manners," observed the American author and philosopher Ralph Waldo Emerson, "are made up of petty sacrifices." This quaint notion no doubt appealed to his nineteenth-century audience; can you think of many aphorisms less likely to appeal to the modern mind?

We live in an era that is profoundly antithetical to the idea of sacrifice. Oh, in theory, in principle, in *public*, we are all in favor of manners, and agree wholeheartedly that there should be more of them—especially among other people.

But manners require a range of attributes that are deeply unfashionable today. Patience. Self-control. Awareness of others. Deferral of self-gratification. A readiness to make those small Emersonian sacrifices. A preparedness to comply with rules that are less than ideal or may, in truth, seem rather silly.

And while we may appreciate that rare young fellow who holds out his elbow to little old ladies, queues placidly at the bank, turns off his phone in restaurants, abides uncomplainingly by the road rules and waits patiently for his colleagues to finish their sentences; while we may even admire him, as one delights at a glimpse of a shy rare bird, we are unlikely to whisper in awe to ourselves: *There's a man whose destiny lies at the top!* An amplitude of manners, far from being to our young man's advantage, may well suggest to us that he lacks the egoistic aggression necessary to win the Darwinian contest of modern life.

The irony is that once—not so very long ago—such fine behavior would have communicated to observers an aura of obvious strength. For a thousand years, good manners in Western civilization were regarded as the very emblem of social and political authority. Etymology draws the link: the word *courtesy* takes its origins from the European court system, just as *chivalry* relates to the officer class that rode horses into battle. Indeed, manners were not only inculcated as a virtue, they were an active means to demonstrate superiority. That's why *noblesse* was rather inclined to *oblige.*

And, now that I think of it, there's still another problem.

This is a time of big and important words. Globalization and terrorism and fundamentalism and climate change. As Emerson reminds us, manners are just so, well, so petty. It's hard not to feel that there is something meager about arguing the case for cell phone etiquette when the planet is hotting up, the Middle East is imploding, terrorists plot our demise and much of Africa is starving. It's hard not to wonder if, among the grand and awe-inspiring issues of our day, manners must come a long way down the list.

And perhaps it's partly for this exact reason that I am interested in the humble and concrete topic of everyday civility. Manners are one of the few things each of us has under our own control. No slogans, no outsize goals, no unrealistic ambitions. An arena of life in which we can all effect some tangible if tiny benefit.

And yet, and yet . . .

Surely manners are much more than a minor phenomenon in daily life? After all, they reflect the values of the society from which they spring and they influence the direction that society will take. Manners matter, though not because they are an absolute good in themselves. Of course they are not. But they sit at the nexus of some of our most fundamental challenges.

Daily we wrestle with these human dilemmas: the choice between seizing our moment and waiting our turn; imposing our judgments and accepting the edicts of others; making a noise and holding our tongues; advancing our immediate interests and promoting the broader good. We are constantly making these fine and complex calibrations.

We must each of us discover: what do we owe ourselves and what do we owe the community in which we live and work and make our lives? How do we juggle this conundrum of self and society?

Manners are a civil mode of human interaction. They matter because they represent an optimal means to preserve our own dignity and the dignity of others. So when we give way to others, when we keep our temper, when we help someone old or frail—these individual gestures, seemingly so small, add up to the not inconsiderable achievement of a civil society. Our small sacrifices amount to something big.

There are manners, and then there are *beautiful* manners. These don't merely preserve everyone's dignity; they actively enlarge the social space. Drawing the shy guest into wider conversation. Sending a thank-you note. Going the extra step to help a stranger wearily tugging their heavy bags. Beautiful manners expand the radius of human cooperation and potential. I think that's why witnessing a gracious gesture can unexpectedly fill us with joy.

Much has been said and written about manners in recent times. Lamentations for their decline. Exhortations to improve. Even handbooks on modern manners, many of which gamely attempt to guide us through the myriad new opportunities that the modern office, urban consolidation, sexual freedom, information technology and congested traffic have created for us to be incredibly uncivil to one another.

Such books may have value, but this is not one of them.

This essay explores the case for manners. It stems from a sense that each generation must defend civilized behavior against the human tendency to regress to barbarism. It tries to understand how manners connect us to things we cherish,

5

such as health, freedom, order, progress, community and authenticity. It seeks to illuminate how manners beneficially shape the ways we nurture our individual humanity, and how we construct and preserve our wider communities. I can't promise, however, that it will have the wit to answer the question posed by a canny four-year-old to her perplexed aunt: "But *why* can't we say 'fuck' at preschool?"

And it is offered with the hope that perhaps, if we were to take a positive interest in manners—if we were in a position to devote our attention to this subject beyond arguing about the basic rules or railing against those who break them—we might even find ourselves concerned with higher things. We might even, who knows, find ourselves engaged in a discussion about the true nature of citizenship and a democratic aesthetics of living.

Because if the idea of civilization matters at all, then so do manners. At least, such is the case I hope to make in the following pages.

Because man is an animal

I WAS TWENTY YEARS OLD when I first visited the Renaissance city of Florence. Like so many others before me, I felt an immediate affinity as I walked the streets. After the grandeur of Rome, small-scale Firenze seemed intimate, approachable. *Human.*

And somewhat surprisingly, for I am not a particular fan of sculpture, one moment above all others has stayed with me. One image, one experience, one sense-memory. It was when I visited the Accademia and tilted back my head to take in Michelangelo's statue of David: when my eyes rolled up seventeen marbled feet of perfection.

Completed in 1504, *David* embraces the most moving contradictions: young boy and virile adult; vulnerable nude and godlike figure; flesh-and-blood animal and magnificent man; private contemplation and heroic action. To gaze at *David* is to apprehend what it means to be human, with all its fragility and soaring possibility.

Which was exactly Michelangelo's point.

Michelangelo and the other leaders of the Renaissance had internalized a big idea. Having rediscovered the glories of the ancient Greeks, they believed that not only were there more things on heaven and earth than the teachings of the all-dominant Catholic Church, but that man was capable of finding them out. Copernicus unveiled the golden revolutions of the sun. Leonardo imagined helicopters whirring through the air. Columbus climbed down from his sailing ship and stumbled onto America. Just as important, Gutenberg with his printing press found a way to disseminate this new learning to ordinary people.

The genius of the Renaissance was to assert that man was not a degraded shadow cowering in the eyes and image of God but an autonomous, questing, dauntless creature. Like Michelangelo's *David*.

So it may come as a surprise to discover that one of the key preoccupations of the Renaissance was farting.

It was in 1530 that Erasmus of Rotterdam, known forever after as Wise Erasmus, published his little book—really a booklet more than a book—called *De Civilitate Morum Puerilium*, or *On Civility Among Boys*. In it, Erasmus addressed his

8

advice on behavior to the flesh-and-blood equivalents of Michelangelo's marvelous boy. It was an instant and massive best seller. Twelve editions were printed in 1530 alone. For 150 years this handbook spread across Europe—translated into English in 1532 and reprinted in 1534, 1540 and 1554; German in 1536, French and Czech in 1537; Swedish in 1620; Dutch in 1660; and Finnish in 1670. Curious how late the Finns came to modern manners.

And to read this little book is still a pleasure, for it is sane and tolerant and funny and wise. I like to imagine Erasmus during his travels in Italy looking up at Michelangelo's *David*, that delicate and muscular hand, those marble curls, those ripples of thigh and rib and buttock, that tender penis. I like to think of him rubbing his chin and saying to himself, *Mmm, yes, very nice. But none of the lads I know match up to that marbled perfection. My boys are human, all too human.*

That is to say, still animals. For many of Erasmus's injunctions revolved around the management of bodily functions. He issued clear and uncomplicated guidelines for the civil young man:

> FARTING: *Don't squeeze your buttocks to prevent the emission as it may injure your health, so if you must in company, cover with a discreet and well-timed cough.*
>
> BAD BREATH: *Rinse your mouth out every morning.*

SNEEZING: *Turn away, and graciously accept a Bless You.*

YAWNING: *Cover your mouth and then make the Sign of the Cross.*

BELCHING: *Some people do it after every third word—this is disgusting.*

NOSE BLOWING: *Best to use a handkerchief, don't trumpet like an elephant, turn away, never wipe your nose on a sleeve, and if you must blow into your fingers resulting in some mucus hitting the dirt, for heaven's sake grind it in with your foot.*

This is a fine example of Renaissance humanism at its best. Civilization wasn't just about raising heroic buildings and making extraordinary scientific discoveries. The emphasis on manners was a way to embrace man's higher aspirations for a civilized life while simultaneously exerting control over his lowest animal functions.

One rarely likes to be reminded that one is an animal. But it must plainly be accepted that while Botox may have eliminated the wrinkle, no one, to my knowledge, has yet eradicated the burp. The tummy rumble. The snotty winter nose. The excruciating squelchy noises that occur during sex. Amazing: we are now capable of cloning our own body parts, but we haven't yet found a way to suppress the uncontrollable urge to cough during the dramatic pause in a play. Or to silence the echoing booms of a diarrhea attack in a thin-walled holiday cottage shared with new friends you were once hoping to impress—but now hope never to see again.

In our modern world we confront a paradox. In certain circles the human body is increasingly looking like the product of a laboratory experiment conducted by a sexual deviant: ageless and lineless and unmarked and plumped up and thinned down and resculpted. Science is helping us to suppress nature. But even the most exquisite Hollywood specimen can never entirely overcome the bodily realities. As Montaigne, a French admirer of Erasmus, once observed, "Upon the highest throne in the world, we are seated, still, upon our arses . . ."

I thought longingly of Erasmus not long ago as I sat in the back of a cab while the driver hawked and sniffed and comprehensively, indeed luxuriantly, gargled his sputum before spitting a great gelatinous yellow gob sideways out his window onto the street. And I think of him regularly when I see teams of Australian cricketers or American baseball players issuing a seemingly endless stream of expectorant from their lips onto playing fields and ballparks—in front of thousands of admiring fans and a global TV audience.

Someone should inform those sportsmen that social injunctions against spitting are not a capricious imposition on their oral freedoms. They are not a cruel and arbitrary assault on baseball's romantic baccy-chewing traditions. They are a pragmatic issue of germ management.

I was reminded of this in a most alarming way last year when I visited my father in a public hospital. It was one of those brutalist 1950s buildings with long, ominous linoleum corridors. To add to the air of doom, my father's kidney ward was on the same floor as the psychiatric emergency unit. My brother and I emerged from the elevator to be met by a glassy-eyed man dressed in a hospital gown with bandages around his throat and wrists. Our carefully upbeat smiles faltered a little. But this was by no means the worst.

Along the corridors, at the elevator, near the nurses' station, was a series of signs reminding staff to be careful of hygiene and *wash your hands*. Above the sink was a sign with simple pictures showing the staff exactly how to do this. *Don't forget those thumbs!* appeared to be the message. And outside my father's ward was another sign, actively encouraging visitors to remind those forgetful nursing staff of their hygienic obligations. "Jesus," my brother said. We felt it was wise not to mention this apparent ignorance of basic cleanliness to our fragile patient lest it further delay his recovery.

If even professional nursing staff have to be reminded that hygiene is a good thing—and shown on the job how to perform this most basic task—no wonder athletes feel no obligation to swallow their spit.

Whenever we suppress a cough in public, cover our mouths when we sneeze, stay home from work if we are sick, wash our hands before handling food, wear deodorant, bathe or shower regularly, eat with our mouths closed—when we do these things, we are not simply rehearsing mindless rituals.

We are doing nothing less than contributing to our own survival and that of the species.

. . . a social one

Of course, we are more than just any old animal: man is a social animal.

Human social life is, thankfully, more sophisticated than an ant colony or a beehive. We have progressed beyond assigning permanent, fixed roles to our members. We use our higher faculties to go beyond a mere eating and breeding program. We have learned how to ameliorate weakness and rectify unfairness.

But the simple reality is that each one of us relies upon the cooperation and collaboration of others for our survival. We need each other. Not just the people we know and rely upon for life's necessities, like our forbearing general medical practitioner or the chef at our favorite Thai restaurant. But even people we don't know, and definitely wouldn't like, including the fellow blasting the neighborhood with his leaf blower, or the driver who won't let you into her lane when you need to turn off at the next exit, or the marketing operative who calls to demand your opinion of his company's product just as you are finally sitting down to your first gin and tonic of the day.

Even when we don't want to answer the phone, we are all still connected.

Animals develop instinctive methods to do this. But we humans are forced to use our reason and our sense and our goodwill to figure out what works and what doesn't at each point in our history. There is an innate beauty in the workings of the animal world. We self-conscious creatures have to go a step further to make life beautiful.

Manners are neither authentic nor spontaneous. They are constructed and invented. Artificial. Made up. Like traffic lights. Air-traffic control regulations. Court procedures. Parliamentary rules. Football rules. They may be imperfect, but they are nevertheless a means to direct human traffic in an orderly fashion. They are about making things work.

And when we get it right, we really do make things better.

Not so long ago, I sat at dinner next to a clever man who works with computers. He described to me a future in which our appliances will form a sort of network to look after us— our fridge, phone, car, personal computer, air conditioner, TV and music system will all be in close touch, sorting things out, making things work. No, you can't ask me how.

I immediately began looking forward to the day when I won't have to feel inadequate because I am incapable of utilizing any more than 2 percent of the capacity of any of my appliances: when the future arrives my appliances will have worked out how to be 100 percent useful to me all by themselves. I was even more amazed to discover that the way this will happen is by a sort of computerized version of manners.

It seems that the terminology of manners has been fully incorporated into all the digital technologies. The Internet is chock-full of *protocols*: standardized sets of rules governing the exchange of data between given devices. Programmers talk about *etiquette*. They even refer to *handshaking*. Alarming to think that our machines might wind up being more polite than our work colleagues. And of course, as systems evolve, so digital manners will evolve, as well. One day soon my car and my fridge will metaphorically bow to each other as they exchange information about the gaps in my food supply, what items should be automatically reordered from the supermarket for home delivery and what fresh items I need to buy on my way home.

Who would ever have thought computer programmers would be at the forefront of civilization? By the end of this conversation I had a delightful vision of a not-very-distant future in which manners might be integrated advantageously into all aspects of our lives.

But then I remembered dismally that overall we seem to be losing our gift for mutually beneficial interaction. Many of us find going out into the world so trying that it seems easier to avoid it altogether. It appears altogether less stressful to the nervous system to stay at home where one can exert at least partial control over the environment.

And when we do leave home, driven by the overwhelming need to earn a living or go to the January sales or eat good Italian food, our apprehension about what we might encounter in the world proves to be negatively reinforcing. We put on our dark glasses and avoid eye contact. Increasingly we plug in our iPods: less for tuning into the music than tuning out the people around us. We talk or text on our cell phones constantly, on the train or bus, in the shops and cinemas, on the street. It's as if we deprive ourselves of immediate sensory stimulation—shade our eyes, block our ears, stop our mouths—in order to experience the world through a protective mask.

Finally, when with reluctant resignation we do interact with a stranger—with, say, a taxi driver or a coffee barista or a checkout person at the supermarket—we do it all with sign language and half sentences, often still talking on the phone to someone (anyone!) else as if to distract our attention away from the irritations inherent in any physical, material encounter with untested individuals. People we need, and upon whose goodwill we depend.

In our efforts to avoid all the latent rudeness and unpleasantness in the world, we, too, have become harder, and ruder, and less pleasant. Yet the more we distrust each other, the more we are confused and irritated by each other, the greater the risk that we abandon the task of finding a common language with which to peacefully interact.

In my block of units there's a different but connected problem. We share the same building, we see each other regularly, we pass close by each other in the foyer and on the stairs. But because we don't have manners, we have no formula for successfully relating to each other. Living in the noisy hubbub of the city, each one of us wants to protect our privacy, especially at home. Me, too. I consider myself something of an urban hermit. I don't want to be friends with people purely because we live in close proximity. On the other hand, it's rather strange to pretend you have no knowledge of someone who lives across the hall.

So when we cross paths we all shift our eyes or mumble *Hi*—but it's awkward. No one wants to cross that dreaded threshold into cozy familiarity or, God forbid, mutual obligation. Here is where manners would come in handy. In a more mannered world we'd simply get the introductions over with, have a cup of tea and then return to pleasant but formal distance. *Good morning. Lovely day, isn't it?* we would say. But instead we scuff and shuffle and we're not sure whether to smile or not and the whole process is uncomfortable. The fear of overfamiliarity with our neighbors has led to an inability to relate to each other in any way at all.

Which is weird, because we all live very close together

indeed. The irony of our routine of nonrecognition is brought home to me every Friday night as I lie in bed with the breeze drifting through the window. That's when the circus nearby begins again.

It starts with a male falsetto. *How dare you!* Operatic intake of breath: *How daaaare you!*

And: *Don't you ever, ever say that to me again!*

Then, hoarsely: *Get out, get out, damn you!*

After an interval, sniveling: *Oh no, you're not going, are you? Don't leave me, don't leave me!*

Then later, *Oh, Robert, Robert!* in manly tones.

So much for privacy. If we all knew our manners, we could live with our neighbors more comfortably. We could know just enough about them, but not too much. People might think a mannered world sounds cold and lonely. But when you have no manners at all it becomes almost impossible to relate to people in a functional way. And that can be lonely, too.

We are proud individuals and we are social animals. Manners help us resolve our double identities.

. . . with a habitat to protect

Here's a funny coincidence: declining standards of civility and the looming crisis of global warming. At first glance, no two things could appear to be less connected. But let's tease out this extravagant thought and see where it leads.

As wealth increases and standards of civility decline, we know that more and more people are retreating from society and investing in their own private domains: the forecasters and marketers call this trend *cocooning*.

When the outside world seems difficult and unpleasant, family homes become essential domains for personal autonomy and a sense of *personal space*. In some households, the breakdown in civility extends even to interactions between family members. The parents then build a separate *parents' retreat* to get away from their children. The teenagers get their own private wing. By creating these disparate spaces, intergenerational incivilities can be avoided, except for the occasional gruff encounter at the fridge or, once in a while, the dinner table. Separate bathrooms are a must, to prevent the stresses of forming and managing a queue. And so houses get bigger and bigger for fewer people.

And now the family seeks to replicate privately the pleasures that once would have been sought communally. The private pool replaces the beach or public pool. The wide-screen TV obviates the discomforts of the cinema. Computers and games are installed so that the children can play variations on the cops-and-robbers games that they might once have played out on the streets with the other neighborhood kids. BBQ equipment and outdoor facilities eliminate the need to visit the local public park.

The family is increasingly preserved against society, instead of in concert with it.

To facilitate most of these pleasures the temperature needs to be constant—so air-conditioning is installed. This has the secondary benefit of blocking out the noise from the neighbors. And of course, all family members prefer to travel by car rather than by rail or bus. Preferably separate cars, as a matter of fact. And ideally, enormous fuel-consuming four-wheel-drive vehicles to insulate the occupants as far as possible from the hurly-burly of commuter traffic.

These measures not only contribute to the decline in communal living, they greatly expand each individual's environmental footprint.

Very rich people have additional choices at their disposal. Indeed, one of the great perceived advantages of prosperity in this modern era is the prospect of separating yourself from other people: to flee from the madding crowds with their ugly and importunate ways. Private yachts and planes provide an energy-inefficient bubble of personal comfort to transport the wealthy to exclusive boutique hotels in hard-to-reach hideaways. Remote destinations, away from it all, untouched by human hands. This, too, has environmental implications as large tracts of land are cleared to provide privacy and comfort for a small number of people.

Of course, the behavior of a relatively small group of people will have little bearing on the problems of climate change or their solution. Indeed, it may well be that there are aspects of *cocooning*, like online shopping, that actually contribute to energy efficiency rather than its opposite. But it is a statement of fact that when we shrink from society into our private worlds, when the breakdown in civility backs us further and further into our own corners, we each consume more of the planet's scarce resources.

In our heart of hearts, of course, we must know it won't work. There is no escape from the humanity bath. We are all in it: up to our necks in it.

As we embark on our global emergency mission to save the environment, is it too much to ask whether we might also find ourselves incidentally creating a more cooperative and civil world?

Or, to put it another way: Wouldn't it be something if civility helped save the planet?

2

Because manners are more important than laws

IN OUR OWN TIME, the idea that petty old manners are more important than laws may seem unthinkable, possibly even undemocratic. But in November 1789, the English parliamentarian Edmund Burke received a letter. A young French politician sought his views on recent dramatic developments in Paris. At that time the French Revolution was only a few months old and many of Burke's countrymen regarded the humbling of the French monarch and the humiliation of the Catholic Church as a cause for celebration. *Liberty was on the move!* And surely it would spread like a ray of light across Europe.

Burke himself was a liberal and a modernizer. He believed in tolerance, progress and the vital role of Parliament in good national governance. He'd even gone so far as to criticize the

British king over his stubborn mismanagement of colonial policies in America, India and Ireland.

But Burke was deeply worried about the French Revolution. And once he started writing, he couldn't stop. What began as a simple letter turned into a two-hundred-page polemic. *Reflections on the Revolution in France* deplored the Revolution, predicted its calamitous course and put forward Burke's notions about the ways in which a sane society should protect itself from extremism.

Burke was not a natural ally with the past and conservatism and the old aristocratic values. But he saw that by overthrowing the monarchy and the Catholic Church and by nationalizing church properties, even in the name of Liberty, the Revolution was effectively wiping out the two primary sources of French manners. And he was extremely apprehensive about what might appear in their place.

Burke understood what history later proved—that radical revolutionaries are nearly always authoritarians in disguise:

> . . . *[T]hese pretended citizens treat France exactly like a country of conquest. . . . The policy of such barbarous victors [is] . . . to destroy all vestiges of the ancient country, in religion, in polity, in laws and in manners; to confound all territorial limits, to produce a general poverty; to put up their properties to auction; to crush their*

princes, nobles and pontiffs; to lay low everything which had lifted its head above the level, or which could serve to combine or rally, in their distresses, the disbanded people, under the standard of old opinion.

Throughout the rest of his life, Burke kept returning to the vital connection between culture, society, civilization—and manners. In 1796, in his *Letters on a Regicide Peace*, Burke gave his fullest and most famous statement on the subject:

Manners are of more importance than laws. Upon them, in a great measure, the laws depend. The law touches us but here and there, and now and then. Manners are what vex or soothe, corrupt or purify, exalt or debase, barbarise or refine us, by a constant, steady, uniform, insensible operation, like that of the air we breathe in. They give their whole form and colour to our lives. According to their quality, they aid morals, they supply them, or they totally destroy them.

The logic of Burke's thinking is powerful. Manners are both evidence of a functioning society and an important means to uphold that society. Manners provide a form of social self-limitation, a means by which citizens signal their willingness to live together and to abide by common standards. Legislate all you like, but laws can never have the same socially binding effect as manners, which give their *whole form and color* to our lives. Destroy manners—sweep aside all of a society's habits, conventions and patterns of behavior—and you may well find you have nothing left but chaos. And because human beings cannot live for long in a state of anarchy, sooner or later some form of oppressive authority will step in to restore order on new, more punitive premises.

Burke's predictions were amazingly accurate. The French revolutionaries quite literally decided to destroy the existing order and start again from scratch. Year Zero. The old aristocracy was thrown out, and property rights, and the church, and French history and all the old ways and manners. In came a new calendar complete with new days and months, new secular gods and goddesses and feast days, new terms of social address—in short, a whole new world was brought into being by edict. And the intoxicating exercise of legislative power didn't end there, because the Jacobin extremists under Robespierre instituted a brief but terrifying orgy of death. The Terror—lasting from 1792 to 1794—would become the first experiment in modern totalitarianism, providing the radical template for tyrants like Stalin in Russia and Mao in China. And still that wasn't the end of the story, because in 1799 Napoleon Bonaparte stepped up to impose a military dictatorship on an exhausted and somewhat relieved France.

The revolutionary zeal to achieve liberty, equality and fraternity had resulted in the sustained triumph of oppression.

In Burke's mind, manners were not a peripheral question. If you cared about civilization, you cared about manners.

⚜

Rule of law is a beautiful thing. And legislation has been used to great positive effect, both to reflect changing social attitudes and to accelerate a shift in behaviors. But you simply can't dictate all our human behaviors without enslaving us. The equation is ultimately simple: more laws, more police, more lawyers equals less civilization.

That's why it is alarming to note that there has never in the history of the Western world been as much legislation as there is today. This explosion of laws could legitimately be regarded as a sign of social failure: either the state is attempting overly to restrict its citizens, or we citizens are simply no longer capable of regulating ourselves. This phenomenon is not just a function of new technologies and a more complex world, though that's part of it.

You can be sure it's a problem when even the lawyers—the main beneficiaries of this trend—despair at the infectious spread of legislation. In 2005, the president of the New South Wales Law Society, John McIntyre, gave a speech in which he lamented the proliferation of laws in Australia. McIntyre asked: "Surely human relationships have not undergone such a dramatic change in thirty years that their regulation by government now demands the attention of numerous Acts of Parliament, including the Family Law Act and Rules which total in excess of a massive 1,000 pages?"

If we look at something as basic as the road traffic laws in any Western country, we can see that they have mushroomed, multiplied, grown wild. Gone from pamphlets to door-stoppers. Expanded and bulged. I guess it's inevitable. Because if you can't achieve driving harmony through manners and good sense, then you try to achieve the same result through laws. More and more and more of them. McIntyre posed the question: "Is driving a motor vehicle in 2005 so different to driving in 1973 that it requires not 20 sections, but 351 road rules?"

But the size of the bits of paper is not the main problem. You only have to walk out onto the street to see people blithely breaking the law every day: jaywalking, littering, running red lights, talking on their cell phones while driving, revving their engines, honking their horns, emitting strident music, tailgating the cars in front of them. All ill-mannered and all illegal. These breaches are rarely enforced and, indeed, are largely unenforceable, unless we were to create a police state.

So we don't have manners. Nor do we have laws that are enforced. We do, however, have road rage. And a generalized sense of despair and apathy because the system doesn't seem to be working.

In 2003, the city of New York mounted a legislative campaign against rudeness. Years of pleading simply hadn't worked with those recalcitrant New Yorkers: it was time to get tough. The mayor, Michael R. Bloomberg, imposed a smoking ban, overhauled the city's noise code and decreed that parents could be ejected from Little League games for unsportsmanlike behavior. Subway riders who rested their feet on a seat were liable to pay a $50 fine. It became illegal for fans to interfere with professional sports events by invading the field or molesting the players. The laws received widespread media coverage and praise.

But here's the catch. When I last checked, the $50 fine on people who used their cell phones during movies, concerts and Broadway shows had never, apparently, been enforced by police.

Some commentators have said that the mere enactment of the law is, of itself, sufficient to revise behavior by signaling broad community attitudes. I have some sympathy with this view. But it risks a more dangerous problem. When too many laws are not enforced, are not *enforceable*, the danger is not only that you diminish the authority of that particular law, but that you diminish the very power and reputation of the law itself.

Of course, in our unmannered era, laws must seem like an appealing shortcut to achieve social harmony. After all, laws can be rapidly produced: they are simply the product of a conversation in a parliament. Manners take time to catch on. They are delicate and subtle things, relying upon broad agreement and usage, shaped by circumstances, molded by collaborative effort.

And it seems to me there *is* a useful role that civic authorities can play in reflecting and shaping communal standards of manners, but through the employment of charm rather than legal menace. In January 2007, for example, *The New York Times* reported on a campaign by the local transit authority of Paris to improve standards of courtesy. Rather than threaten prosecution, the Parisians decided instead to install humorous posters to persuade commuters to muzzle their pets, refrain from littering, talk softly on cell phones, avoid whacking their neighbors with their backpacks—and to say a pleasant hello and goodbye to their bus drivers.

Such modest education measures seem to me far more useful than the sledgehammer of laws. They give moral reinforcement to the courteous commuters as well as useful correctives to the rude ones.

Imagine how awful life would be if we relied solely upon laws to enforce all decent behavior. In such circumstances, we would be no better than robots. We would be incapable of freely exercising and receiving kindness and courtesy. We would be less than ourselves.

That's why we need the collective endowment, the community collaboration, the unmistakable signs of a coherent, free civilization conferred by the voluntary gift of manners.

. . . less invasive than morals

There's a long tradition that manners are a matter of ethics; that for guidance on manners we should be able to rely upon our shared moral sense and codes. And I agree with this, up to a point.

But there's a problem.

We live in pluralist societies, and they're only getting more diverse. They are multiracial. They are multireligious. We can no longer assume a common Judeo-Christian upbringing to draw us all automatically together. Once, we could confidently agree to do unto others as we would have done unto us because we could roughly agree on what we would—and would not— like done. But today even the differences between the generations are now so significant that advertising agencies have invented different code names for us—gray nomads, baby boomers, Gen X, Gen Y—as if we are separate species of human, which sometimes it appears as though we are.

So it no longer makes sense to exhort us to draw upon our shared moral codes. Because what might seem kind and considerate to you might irritate me. Or what might seem completely inconsequential to me might desperately hurt your feelings. Indeed, we seem to have brought ourselves to the point where we have few confidently agreed upon rules for social engagement at all. Is it okay if I take this call during our meeting? Will they be offended if I am twenty minutes late? How about if I text-message at the dinner table?

Most of the time, in these uncertain conditions, we rationally conclude in favor of our immediate interests rather than in support of some obscure or uncertain social good. We take the call. We turn up late. We send and receive the text messages. And so the cycle of ill manners continues—leaving many people feeling offended, frustrated, impotent and confused.

While for most of us this is all deeply unpleasant, there are some who sniff an opportunity in social instability. Fundamentalists and ideologues—no matter what their beliefs— favor strict rules, unvaryingly applied, admitting neither flexibility of interpretation nor adaptation to circumstance. Which wouldn't matter a bit except they tend not to limit their views to how they themselves should behave. They have strong opinions about how the rest of us should behave, as well. And they'd like to impose them upon us.

In the twentieth century, fundamentalist idealists like communists and Nazis had a total worldview and were able to impose those views on societies that were simultaneously chaotic and weary enough to embrace them. I lived in the then communist city of Belgrade for a period and saw for myself that nothing erodes manners like the common ownership of the means of production. Power to the people had produced a society that was sullen, unkind and competitive.

Now we have an upsurge in religious fundamentalism, with evangelists of various kinds admonishing us to model our actions strictly on the guidelines of some or other unhappy Middle Eastern fellow who lived and died a long time ago. But it seems to me these strictures have a very limited utility for the moral or practical conduct of modern life.

It's not, of course, that fundamentalists aren't sincere. On the contrary, it's possible to sincerely hold really horrible thoughts, feelings and values. Racists tend to be sincere. Bigots are sincere. Fundamentalist Muslims and Jews are sincere. And fundamentalist Christians, guided by their comprehensive moral system, are perfectly sincere in trying to impose their vision of God's Kingdom on Earth upon everyone else. But the problem is this: fundamentalists don't just want to tell me what to do when I am out in public. They are unnervingly keen on interfering in my private domain, as well. Coming into my home and telling me how to conduct my romantic life or marriage; poking into my bedroom and pronouncing pruriently on my sex life; even telling me how to dispose of my own body.

Take, for example, death. Surely a personal matter if ever

there was one. It seems to me that while manners are clearly very useful for living, they might come in handy for dying, too. Should I be terminally ill, I like the idea of arranging an orderly departure. One that is well-organized and causes the minimum of physical pain to me and emotional pain to those who care for me. An exit plan that is strictly my choice. And if, by sad fate, I were no longer able to be myself—if I were in a permanent coma, or profoundly demented, or in agonizing pain, or experiencing extreme disability—then I would like my husband to have the right to end my life. (He likes that idea, too, I note with mixed feelings.) In such circumstances, it would seem to me not only cruelly pointless but rather bad manners to go on living, particularly if only by costly artificial means—rather like overstaying my welcome at a dinner party by fifteen or twenty years. And it irritates me that extremists presume bossily to interfere with a process that surely only an extreme optimist would deny was inevitable, and peculiar to me alone.

In short, I would very much prefer not to have anyone use their moral system as an excuse to impose limitations on my personal freedoms, when the exercise of those personal freedoms inflicts no social harm.

Give me manners, by contrast, that ensure the minimum intrusion on my rights and privacy; that adapt flexibly to social evolution; that do not presume; that protect everyone's rights and dignities; and that contribute ever so gently to the social good.

Indeed, it seems to me that the person who operates in the world on the basis of manners is far less likely to do harm than the God-botherer, fundamentalist, sexist, racist or other morally driven individual.

Manners are a way to render very diverse people acceptable to each other. If we accept that a single arbitrary and sweeping code of morals can no longer bind our varied society together, perhaps manners might pragmatically take its place.

And perhaps, in their low-key way, contribute to a happier society than any perfect ideology could ever achieve.

. . . and better than social confusion

Of course, you are thinking, it's all very well declaring that manners are a terrific idea and more pragmatic than laws or moral systems at shaping a civil society. But how on earth do we establish effective terms and conditions for modern manners?

Excellent question. And you would be perfectly justified in additionally asking whether I would be a person qualified to answer it. I must admit that I find myself writing about manners not because I enjoy mulling over the trivial details of everyday life but precisely because I don't. I dislike it. The truth is, I'd rather not be thoughtful—it requires too much thought. I don't care to be considerate—that requires too much consideration. And those who know me well would confirm, with unflattering speed, that I'm not thoughtful or considerate, not very.

And yet, like most of us, I hunger for civility. At the very least, I want predictability in my human dealings. I like to know what I am entitled to expect from others and from myself. But often I don't know. Everyday interactions feel more like complicated negotiations. I waste more and more emotional energy simply getting through the minutiae of daily life.

The truth is, I gain no enjoyment from pondering who should send the last email in an email exchange (can we stop now?).

I don't find pleasure in wondering whether I can, with propriety, hang up on someone who puts me on call waiting (is it ruder of them to keep me waiting, or of me to hang up after they've kept me hanging?).

And I experience active irritation weighing up whether I can leave the café if the person I am due to meet hasn't shown up, say, twenty minutes after the agreed upon time (if so, will I be the one required to ring and apologize?).

These situations are infuriating and, worse still, boring. They are matters of negligible import, yet to arrive at the right solution requires weighing up various options and carefully selecting among them.

Does not modern life already have far too many options? Options for how we live, who we have sex with, what we wear, what we believe in? Perhaps some people find this freedom of choice liberating.

Me, I don't like it. I don't like all this choice. I don't want to think about which phone provider will deliver me the best combination of prices for the time of day, longevity and distance of my phone calls. I don't care to fret about which yogurt to select given the choice between biodynamic, low-fat, Greek, acidophilus, vitamin-enriched, without gelatin and with honey.

And there is a high chance that, even after the best efforts at wise deliberation, we'll still get it wrong—whether about phone companies or yogurt, or even on matters of courtesy. After all, some of the most painful situations in modern life occur not because people want to be rude, but because they just aren't sure how to behave.

Suppose, for example, a polite young man stands up for a woman on a crowded train. He does so in an automatic kind of way, but if pressed to explain his motives, he might explain that he's noticed she is carrying a very heavy bag and if she sits down she can rest it on her lap. And anyway, he doesn't mind standing as he is getting off soon and she looks really tired and his mum always encouraged him to be kind to people.

It's possible, just possible, that the subject of our young

man's invitation will thank him and graciously take the proffered seat. It's also possible that she will be offended in any variety of ways, and be tempted to think or express thoughts such as:

So that's it. I'm now an old hag. An. Old. Hag. Hang on. That woman under the Exit sign is clearly older than me. Do I look older than her? No, I do not. You. Utter. Bastard.

Or:

Typical. Forty years of feminism and we're back to this. The patriarchy reigns, even among Generation X. Well, I'm not having a bar of it. Piss off.

Or:

Oh God. Does he think I'm pregnant? He thinks I'm pregnant. I knew I should never have bought an empire line.

And this is where all those etiquette books should now come gloriously into their own. Time to whip out the latest manners instruction manual and turn to page 201: *When to stand up on a bus—and how to react when someone offers you a seat.* But I have noticed these books never seem to have a ready answer to the specific question you have in mind.

As a matter of fact, this is the least of their defects. Oh, they are dull. And *long.* And they date so quickly.

Take *Etiquette for Women: A Book of Modern Modes and Manners* (the author, teasingly, identifies herself merely as *One of the Aristocracy*), which dates from 1902 and tells us in no uncertain terms that after you have been invited to a ball, a dinner or a reception, whether the invitation has been accepted or not, you should, as a matter of course, pay *a visit of ceremony* to your hostess within a week, ten days at the latest. It also tells us how to cope with that newfangled development, the restaurant, which, it warns us, is here to stay, despite its troubling implications for the decay of hospitality.

Lady Una Troubridge in the 1920s offers the more upbeat *Etiquette and Entertaining: How to Help You on Your Social Way.* In the bright, modern post–World War I era, Lady Troubridge assures us that the new etiquette is informal. That's presumably why she adjures us to "Let Everything Be Simple" when setting the breakfast table.

All we have to do is:

- Use a spirited check-cloth or a coloured one.
- Arrange the dishes on the sideboard.
- At the head of the table place an encampment of cups round the teapot, milk jug, sugar basin and hot water jug or coffee pot and hot-milk jug.
- At each place put a small fork on the left, and two small knives on the right—the extra knife is to spread butter on bread or toast.
- Set a small plate to the left of the larger plate on which bacon and eggs or some other breakfast dish is served.

- And, because it's an informal meal, the loaf can be on the table as well as the toast-rack, butter, honey and marmalade.

Breakfast made easy.

❦

Amy Vanderbilt shows no interest in simplifying things in her masterwork, *New Complete Book of Etiquette: The Guide to Gracious Living.* Obviously gracious living in 1952 took some doing because this book is 740 pages long. It is indeed full of facts. It is certainly comprehensive. It is great for use as a doorstop on a windy day.

It is also practically useless, as Amy's world of manners has, thankfully, all but disappeared. For example, there's a section on how to address your Chinese gardener or the younger son of a duke. What to wear when fox-hunting. How to avoid errors in conversation and terminology ("high class," she explains witheringly, is one of those phrases that seem to indicate social inferiority in the person uttering it). How to address your envelope when your correspondent is a member of the British House of Commons—and also happens to be a lord. What to wear if you are invited to a Hop at the West Point military academy. It's worth reading this book just to feel delighted at how many problems of manners you are never, ever going to face. At least, you hope not. A couple of sections are timeless, including her advice to parents: "If your children are very young, don't travel with them at all if you can help it."

Etiquette for Australians, revised edition of 1945, is weightily subtitled *Australian Official and Social Life, Government House, The Australian Army, Navy and Air Force and Women's Services. Australian, English and American Titles of Address and Everyday Life.* I rather enjoyed this one for its revelations about the state of Australia in the immediate postwar period. A long section on Farewell Parties suggests that so many of my countrymen were desperate to leave their patch of heaven in the Lucky Country that a whole field of etiquette had to be created to deal with it. (Apparently there are three categories of escapee—those leaving a country district on receipt of a transference or higher appointment to another part of the state or commonwealth; those leaving the commonwealth to take up residence in another country; and those leaving for a trip abroad. No mention is made of the sort of farewell party you should throw for a bankrupt dejectedly quitting town.)

Another section, called Picnic Parties, reiterates, with an air of increasing desperation, the delights of an excursion into the Australian bush: "One of the most delightful features of Australian life! Formalities disappear! A sense of fine comradeship prevails! Happiness and fun!" The end of the section concedes the altogether harsher realities of the great outdoors:

"Don't grumble if the caterpillar from the overhead trees falls into the milk, if the billy tea is smoked, and if the butter melts quickly."

Etiquette for Australians does offer one permanent insight into the Australian psyche. In a long and detailed section, it begs its readers to develop a little sportsmanship. "Don't bawl at the top of your voice or make vulgar gestures at sporting matches," it pleads. "Never rejoice when your opponent makes a bad slip." And it reminds fans and players of a point that still regularly eludes Australian minds: "The decision of the umpire must be accepted."

Today there seem to be more etiquette books than ever on the market. They are variations on the above themes, updated for casual sex and text-messaging. But they remain impossible to scrutinize seriously. Still long. Still dull. Curiously unhelpful. I can't help wondering whether anyone ever reads them. Perhaps they are just given as Christmas gifts to the relatives and friends we consider most likely to need them—who are therefore, it can only be assumed, the very last people who are likely to open and profit from their pages.

⚜

I have a different idea. In a gesture combining laziness and pragmatism, I suggest we forget about big books of rules and compromise on a short set of guidelines. There's a precedent for what I suggest. The lawyers talk about principle-centered law—that is, clear basic rules capable of being readily understood, remembered and flexibly applied to circumstances. The Ten Commandments are a classic example of principle-centered law.

A modern template for manners might have the same memorable simplicity.

How about something like:

1. Keep to the left (or right, depending on jurisdiction).
2. Keep your word, especially about time.
3. Wait your turn.
4. Look after the weak.
5. Obey the laws and regulations, unless you are mounting a campaign of civil disobedience.
6. Watch what you are doing: multitasking is the enemy of manners.
7. Show appreciation for the kind gestures of others; and
8. Most of the time, shut up.

But I'm open to other suggestions. (However, I think you'll find that most public contingencies are covered here, including our young man and his train companion: see points 4 and 7.)

Perhaps "minding one's manners" sounds less civically virtuous than abiding by the letter of the law. "Observing the niceties" certainly lacks the high tone of adhering to the will of the Lord. But manners, so minor, have the unassailable virtue of mitigating subtle yet serious risks to society. Without manners we become vulnerable to the imposition of more legislation. Or we risk having the moral systems of others imposed upon us. The beauty of manners—when everybody knows the accepted rules of behavior—is that we don't have to mean it, or like it, or be moral, or even sincere.

We just have to do it.

3

Because manners nurture our equality

IN 1776, in their Declaration of Independence, the American Founding Fathers laid out exactly why thirteen United States of America would no longer tolerate the colonial domination of Great Britain. Foremost among their reasons? "We hold these truths to be self-evident," they magnificently declared, "that all men are created equal."

And so a great nation was founded. A democracy based on the exhilarating idea of the equality of man.

A little more than fifty years later, a young Frenchman named Alexis de Tocqueville arrived in the thriving young democracy, ostensibly to study its prison system, but in fact to discover what lessons the new world offered the old. Tocqueville came from an aristocratic French family that had been prominent during the ancien régime and had suffered through the successive turmoils of the Revolution, Bonapartism and the Restoration. *Democracy in America* is the long and famous product of his study.

And it is a wide-ranging survey. It traverses everything from the American constitution, judicial system and states' rights versus union rights, to the role of religion, the education system, industrial relations and the love of money. Tocqueville is not afraid to say what he thinks: my favorite chapter heading in the book is in part 3, chapter 17: "How American Society Appears Both Agitated and Monotonous."

But it must be said: while Tocqueville admired many aspects of American life, manners was not one of them. Manners in democracies, he thought, were often coarse, rarely dignified, not well disciplined nor very accomplished. In fact, Tocqueville believed, "Nothing does more harm to democracy than its outer forms of behaviour. Many people who would be willing to put up with its defects cannot tolerate its manners." You suspect on reading this that Tocqueville considered himself among them.

One anomaly Tocqueville noticed above all: equality breeds a yearning for inequality.

In democracies where the differences between citizens are never very great and they naturally become so close that at any moment they can merge in the mass of the community, numerous artificial and arbi-

*trary distinctions are invented to help individuals in their attempt to
remain aloof for fear of being swept along with the crowd . . .*

As Tocqueville knew from experience, in aristocracies, for
better or for worse, certainty prevails in the social order. From
the highest to the lowest, everyone knows their place. Each
person understands to whom they must defer, over whom
they have power and where their social responsibilities lie.
And this social clarity has a calming and dignifying effect
upon manners. In democracies, by contrast, there occurs a
paradoxical effect: social competition is not eliminated, instead it is amplified: "The personal pride of individuals will
always strive to rise above the common level and will hope to
achieve some inequality to their own advantage."

Thus follows a potentially ugly striving for superiority as
individuals seek to accrue advantage at the expense of one another, and therefore their broader society.

What Tocqueville observed may not have completely surprised America's Founding Fathers—from the start they were
genuinely apprehensive about whether America would be
capable of supporting a civil society.

When he was just a fifteen-year-old schoolboy, George
Washington, America's first president, painstakingly wrote out
110 Rules of Civility and Decent Behavior in Company and Conversation.

After his death, these guidelines were published and became a best seller.

John Adams, the second president, was optimistic that good Republican government could positively influence American manners: "It is the Form of Government which gives the decisive Colour to the Manners of the People, more than any other Thing," he said. But even stout Adams had such grave doubts about the merits of his compatriots that he wasn't altogether confident of his own assertion: ". . . there is so much Rascality, so much Venality and Corruption, so much Avarice and Ambition, such a Rage for Profit and Commerce among all Ranks and Degrees of Men even in America, that I sometimes doubt whether there is public Virtue enough to Support a Republic."

Thomas Jefferson, the third president, the man who drafted the most successful founding national statement in world history, was of the view that no matter how strong the laws and constitution of his new country, if manners failed, then his whole society would fail, as well. "It is the manners and spirit of a people which preserve a republic in vigour," he wrote. "A degeneracy in these is a canker which soon eats to the heart of its laws and constitution."

⁕

I saw the "manners and spirit" of my own people in action the other day.

I was standing at the end of a movie queue with my husband, waiting to buy our tickets to see *The Queen*. Though the queue was rather long, the patrons were relaxed and there was a pleasant hum along the line. Along came a couple with whom we were slightly acquainted. We went to greet each other when suddenly the wife darted toward the front of the queue and squeezed through the door into the cinema. Her husband gazed sheepishly at us. After a moment she came back out clutching two tickets. With a satisfied air she stage-whispered to us, "You can bypass the queue and get your tickets at the snack bar!" And with this she took her husband by the elbow, led him past the queue and disappeared triumphantly inside. My husband and I did not take advantage of this quick-witted means to evade the system. We stayed in line, bought our tickets, entered the cinema and found ourselves seated three rows in front of this couple.

There were other options available to this woman. She might, for example, have suggested to cinema management that patrons could form three quick lines instead of one slow one. She might have told all the people in the queue about the waiting snack-sellers, instead of just my husband and me. Or she might have simply stayed in line like us. But I could see in her eyes that she gloried in outsmarting the system. She had generated advantage for herself and her husband. She had proved herself superior to the rest of us. Her reward, I noted without distress, was to watch more advertisements than we did.

And it was ironic that we were all watching *The Queen,* a movie that portrays Queen Elizabeth II of England as a woman almost heroically incapable of taking the easy way out.

All our modern advertising celebrates and indeed encourages this democratic passion for petty social advantage. We are regularly told that if we buy *this* brand of handbag or *that* brand of cell phone we will be just that little bit better than our peers. In fact, that they will no longer be our peers, for we shall have risen a delicious fraction above them.

Consider this advertisement for a Mitsubishi four-wheel drive. A young woman parks the great beast in a tight space between two average-sized cars. But she hasn't room to open her door. Luckily she has the new sunroof feature so she simply climbs out through the top of the 4WD and gaily scrambles down the enormous hood. *Solved!* What the advertisement doesn't do, of course, is solve the problems her action has caused for others—the drivers who return to their cars to discover they can't open their own doors. But this is perhaps the point, for the young lady has not only found a perfect means to advantage herself, she is simultaneously inconveniencing others—a neat way to cap off her automotive and social triumph.

It's a Tuesday midmorning and I am waiting on Platform 9 for the short ride into the city. The train pulls into the station and the doors open. We all stand back as the passengers climb down onto the platform. Or at least, most of us. Because here he is, fidgeting with irritation and stepping from side to side because he wants to get on now. Right now. He can't bear to wait, not even for another second. So he steps forward and up, onto the train, brushing aside a descending mother who is awkwardly maneuvering her stroller with sleeping babe from the train onto the platform, nudging a tired man with a briefcase, dislodging a young bespectacled student. It's not as if he is particularly assertive in his manner. On the contrary, his eyes are averted and his shoulders are angled to minimize his physical impact. He certainly doesn't want to draw attention to himself. But I see him clearly. His silent message to me and to everyone else is abundantly clear. Not for him the ancient courtesy, *after you*. Nor even the cheery and egalitarian, *me, too*. In his case it's definitely, *me first*. And possibly, probably, *and fuck you all*.

Tocqueville's analysis is surely the only plausible explanation for this rudeness—for I assume my traveling companion was bound by various laws of physics to arrive at Town Hall at the same speed as the rest of us. As Tocqueville said of this competitive phenomenon in America: "An American daily refers to the wonderful equality which prevails in the United States. . . . He proclaims out loud his pride on behalf of his country but secretly on his own behalf he feels considerable distress and aims to show he is an exception to the general rule he is advocating."

I can only imagine that my impolite traveling companion was seeking to allay the considerable distress he felt at being one of the vulgar masses traveling on the public transport system. Yes, so many people, manifestly ordinary, trying desperately via petty means to be an exception to the general rule.

Sometimes this mania for status manifests itself in a different way.

I live in an area that is very popular with actors, who are nearly always out of work. That's why, if they are not sitting in a café, they are serving in it. Actually, usually they are doing both, sitting around looking languid and holding their chin at an interesting angle until finally motivated to wander over and ask you what you'd like to drink, rather in the manner of a favor. Having been brought up to visualize themselves as superstars in waiting, the actors simply will not tolerate being treated as waiters, even when that's exactly what they are and are paid to be. Seemingly anxious to remind me that he is better than this, the actor at one local café likes to serve me my coffee while joining in my private conversations, giving his view of the latest film or book or even my menu choice: *I'd go for the penne!* All of which is rarely a prelude to excellent service. Sometimes I feel ashamed of my waiter's shame. I want to tell him about the French professional waiter, who takes such pride in his skill; who abhors overfamiliarity; who feels no nervous compulsion to assert his dignity. I want to say to him: I am not absolutely sure that bad acting would be more honorable than waiting beautifully on tables.

On this matter of social anxiety Tocqueville is particularly insightful when he talks about Americans traveling overseas— and he both prefigures and explains the Ugly American syndrome. As he notes:

When a wealthy American lands in Europe . . . he has such a great fear of being taken for the unsophisticated citizen of a democracy. . . . He is all the more fearful at not receiving the respect due to him because he does not know exactly what governs that respect. . . . He questions every look and carefully analyses all your remarks, lest they contain some hidden allusions to affront him.

American writer Gore Vidal, in his memoir *Point to Point Navigation*, offers us a more contemporary insight into this touchy attitude of mind. As a friend of British Queen Elizabeth's sister Princess Margaret (raffishly referred to by Vidal as PM), Vidal was a guest at a grand party thrown by American businessman Jack Heinz. Vidal and PM were running late, so the queen came over to their pavilion. On being asked by her sister how the party was going, the queen answered ruefully, "We have shaken many hands," indicating that the many American guests had either ignorantly or willfully ignored the protocol that the sovereign should not be touched. Once again, the Americans had gone overboard in their eagerness to be as good as anyone. Or better.

At the end of this little story, Vidal oh-so-casually reminds his readers that he knew exactly the right form: "PM presented me, I did the nod." It seems that even the most patrician American still feels an uneasy compulsion to prove his superiority over his compatriots.

. . . modify self-esteem

But, I regret to advise, there's more. The desire of individuals to rise above the herd was not the only trend that Tocqueville identified as a strong and largely negative feature of democratic society.

He also noted that, as social equality spreads and more people acquire the wealth to satisfy their needs, they progressively retreat from the broader community. Pleased to owe nothing to anyone, they come to expect nothing from anyone, either. This trend toward individualism Tocqueville defined as ". . . a calm and considered feeling which persuades each citizen to cut himself off from his fellows and to withdraw into the circle of his family and friends in such a way that he thus creates a small group of his own and willingly abandons society at large to its own devices."

In order to show that individualism was not necessarily pernicious, Tocqueville contrasted it with egoism, which, he said, was an "ardent and excessive love of oneself that caused people to relate everything to themselves and to prefer themselves above everything."

When I read this section of Tocqueville I did a sort of literary double take. Because at first I couldn't see the real-world difference between citizens cutting themselves off from their fellows and people preferring themselves above everything. Then I realized that I couldn't see the difference between individualism and egoism because in modern life there isn't any. If Tocqueville were to turn up today, I expect he would observe that these formerly separate qualities have now morphed into a single syndrome, whereby people not only embrace utter selfishness but even consider it socially acceptable, if not an active social good. And because we live in an age of misleading euphemisms, we've given this syndrome a palatable and therapeutic label: self-esteem.

Self-esteem is not, of course, a new term. It gained currency in the late nineteenth century as part of the emerging practice of psychology. A body of work emerged suggesting that low self-esteem contributed to individual unhappiness and broader antisocial behavior. I have no doubt the original goals of the self-esteem movement were noble. And I am sure it was once a valuable tool of therapy for the troubled and unhappy.

But where once self-esteem referred to a healthy and unassuming self-confidence, it has now come to represent uncritical self-regard. A campaign that idealizes narcissism. A crusade that encourages people who dislike aspects of themselves to celebrate their shortcomings, rather than to correct them. Self-esteem has become less a neutral descriptor than an active cause.

I looked up *self-esteem* under Amazon books and found 85,962 books devoted to this topic. Among the titles: *The Self-Esteem Workbook. How to Raise Your Self-Esteem: The Proven Action-Oriented Approach to Greater Self-Respect and Self-Confidence. The Self-Esteem Companion. Six Pillars of Self-Esteem. Breaking the Chain of Low Self-Esteem.* And the fast-track version: *Ten Days to Self-Esteem.*

You would think that we were all morally obliged to regard ourselves not only equal by creation but equal in virtue, talent and achievement. How often have I heard someone simpering about their low self-esteem and longed to turn to them and say, "Yes, but perhaps in compensation you have very sound judgment."

Here's an astonishing thing: the self-esteem epidemic breaks the basic rule of civilization—the need to preserve what's best for the group. Self-esteem demands that I am just as important, no, I must regard myself as more important than you. And I must be accommodated no matter how great the inconvenience. And following this cruel logic means that individuals not only demand that others make exceptions for them, but they show no appreciation in return. They feel absolutely no need to connect to their society—it's all and always, just about them. Self-esteem has become the catch-all excuse for putting oneself first all the time.

The consequences are not always minor ones. We, the group, are increasingly at the mercy of:

- The woman who answers her cell phone during a movie and ruins the experience for thirty other people, some of whom no longer feel refreshed by the entertainment but instead emerge from the cinema irritable and take it out on the next-door café waitress, who goes home and cries because her life is so pointless and people are so cruel.

- The parents who insist on allowing their four-year-old to run around the restaurant after 9 P.M., destroying the experience for all the other diners, and especially the tired couple who pulled out their wallets for a babysitter so they could have a rare evening away from their children, and who are now so rattled they don't make love when they get home, which further tests the straining bonds of their marriage.

- The pedestrian who refuses to wait at the lights but insists on walking straight out into the middle of the road, not only risking his own life, but also startling the drivers, holding up the cars and setting in motion a chain reaction of traffic snarls and, three kilometers away, an accident.

- The man who casually drops his cigarette butt on the footpath so it drifts into the great flood tide of rubbish that poisons our waterways, killing off small organisms that are the main food source for a fish that may have certain rare and scientifically valuable enzymes.

- The young man in the elevator who turns to the mirror and spends the journey from the foyer to level 35 grooming himself and treating the public space so egoistically that one of his copassengers, distressed by this annihilating disregard, turns still further in upon herself, and later fails to recognize the unmistakable signs that a work colleague fancies her and loses a chance at happiness.

- The neighbor who thinks it is his perfect right to listen to techno music between 3 A.M. and 6 A.M. after he gets home all hyped-up from a nightclub while around the neighborhood people toss and turn and beat their pillows and finally stagger bleary-eyed and under-slept to their offices the next day where one of them makes a poor decision that loses the company a fortune.

The acid of egoistic individualism has burned deep into our moral and social structures. When *you* behave badly, you are an ill-mannered boor; when I do so, I have good reasons and am completely justified. When *you* jaywalk, you are a self-ish fool; when I do it, it's because the lights have taken too long to change and I'm in a hurry. When *you* take that call, you are an antisocial pig; when I do, it's because it is bound to be very important.

And just as individuals with *self-esteem* never say thank you when you make a courteous concession to them—for, after all, it is their perfect right to do exactly as they please—they get very touchy indeed if you dare to criticize them for any wrongdoing.

True story: in Texas, in 2005, one foolish idealist actually tapped a woman on the shoulder and asked her to stop talking on the phone because she was disturbing the other cinema patrons in the middle of watching a film. The woman immediately had her up on assault charges and the defender of manners was convicted and fined for the crime.

True story: during a Thanksgiving dinner in 2004, two revelers reprimanded another guest for picking at the turkey with his fingers instead of slicing off pieces with a knife. The man responded by taking hold of the carving knife and stabbing them.

This is all, of course, very disheartening. And there's another angle. The flip side of this culture of relentless self-esteem is that to step back, to defer, to make way, is a warning signal of that worst ailment of modern times: *low self-esteem.* Even a simple gesture of courtesy can be misconstrued as a symptom of this sad psychological dysfunction. I've seen parents push their child aggressively forward for fear of what might be said of their parenting techniques if their child is true to his nature and hangs shyly back.

And indeed, it seems to me that parenting is where the worst of the self-esteem epidemic has manifested itself.

The role of children in society has changed. They were once regarded quite literally as the property of their parents and therefore had no rights. Then in a more liberal age, children obtained rights and their parents suddenly had responsibilities. Now it's not so clear. Some parents seem to regard their children as personal investments, to be nurtured and groomed to offer big dividends in terms of parental pride and vicarious achievement. Others seem to have given birth to their new best friends, so their children are alternately placated, indulged and ignored.

But whenever I see parents excessively, duplicitously lavishing praise upon their five-year-old's finger paintings—rather as if the *Mona Lisa* had just emerged magically from those stained and chubby fingertips—I see not another genius-in-waiting but yet another self-esteem monster rising to self-assuredly torment us all in twenty years with an inferior PowerPoint diagram in a marketing meeting.

True story: in January 2007, the American airline AirTran Airways asked a family to leave an aircraft before takeoff when the three-year-old daughter threw a tantrum so severe she could not be persuaded to get into her seat and put on a seat belt. While the parents tried to settle the child, the flight was considerably delayed. But the child absolutely refused to comply, alternately climbing under the seat and emerging to hit her parents. Finally, in accordance with aviation safety rules and in fairness to the other 112 passengers, the crew made an operational decision to remove the family from the aircraft. The mother was utterly dismayed and complained: "We weren't given an opportunity to hold her, console her or anything!" The family assured the media they would never fly AirTran again, a promise of retribution I am fairly certain AirTran contemplated with relief.

I suppose the parents consoled themselves with the knowledge that at least they hadn't wounded the child's developing self-esteem by compulsorily strapping her in like all the other ordinary mortals.

❦

On any Tuesday somewhere near you, you'll find a Rotary Club meeting. Here, accompanied by tepid tea and stewed coffee (if it's a breakfast meeting) or rubber chicken and overcooked spinach (if it's dinner), a strange and well-honed ritual will be played out.

And this ritual will bear a remarkable resemblance to the gatherings of hundreds and thousands of similar groups in countries all around the world. In Australia, we have the St. John Ambulance Brigade and Lions Clubs and Zonta and Probus and Returned Servicemen's Leagues and many more. These private associations serve the interests of their members and, as important, contribute to the common good. The widespread readiness of Americans to participate in such groups (alongside their religion) was, Tocqueville thought, a way the young democracy might successfully mitigate its tendency to individualism in order to create and maintain a civil society.

I must admit, Rotary doesn't look like the kind of place where civilization takes root and flowers.

First there'll be a President John, wearing a big tacky medallion around his neck, who will stand and lead a prayer. The national anthem will then be sung astonishingly badly and with touching gusto. President John will hit a bell with his ancient gavel as a signal to receive the weekly report, notable mostly for its extreme blandness. The secretary will announce in a rapid and monotonous tone the success of past events and the progress of future plans. That achieved, the president will then turn to his lukewarm comic sidekick, probably named Sergeant Ken, who will recount a few innocent jokes downloaded off the Internet and pass around a wooden box to extract "fines" from the joshing but generous members. At the conclusion of the formalities, the Rotarians will sit back in their chairs and dutifully listen to a little talk from a guest speaker about, say, birdwatching or the latest accountancy developments, which will be of almost no interest to anyone, and particularly not to that table of toothless old boys sitting in the corner in the battered navy blue double-breasted jackets they've worn to each and every meeting since 1981.

Most of the time everyone manages to stay awake. But to say there is rarely an atmosphere of excitement is a grave understatement.

Looked at one way—well, truthfully, looked at most ways—Rotary's rituals seem horribly outdated. But whenever and wherever Rotary meets, people are getting things done.

Money is being raised for malaria prevention or sheltering homeless youth. Young people are gaining the opportunity to live overseas and to learn about other cultures.

The manners of Rotary, it turns out, are its strength as well as its weakness. The rituals carry them all through, week after week, year after year. Everyone simply turns up and gets on with business, without fuss or clamor, cushioned by the predictable format. You could fly in from Sri Lanka to a Norwegian chapter of Rotary and you would more or less know what is going on.

Rotary was, for a long time, a very conservative organization. Growing up, we Catholics were rather suspicious of this small businessmen's club, as if it were some kind of antipapist cabal. And yes, Rotary has a conservative air to this day. Some of the more ancient Rotarians still look perturbed when women turn up and take an assertive role.

But last time I was a guest at a Rotary meeting—when I was, in fact, one of those dull guest speakers—I had a sort of mental flash. As I looked around at the Rotary membership—the accountant and the marketing manager and the suburban lawyer and the undertaker—and as they listened to me with courtesy and bought my book and asked after each other's well-being and gave away their money and planned fundraising events and made plans to visit some of their ailing older members, I had a sudden insight that these people were the quiet vanguard of modern civility.

Drawing upon the inexhaustible resource of Rotarian etiquette and a store of personal kindness—without personal vanity or social competitiveness—they were doing nothing less than building a civil world over a cup of tea.

That's why I'll always cherish Rotary, in spite of the rubber chicken.

. . . and connect the self to society

America is the first modern democracy. But it is by no means the only exemplar of a great democracy at our disposal. A very long time ago, in the fifth and fourth centuries before Christ, the Greeks conducted a grand experiment. The historian H.D.F. Kitto frames their story this way: ". . . [I]n a part of the world that had for centuries been civilised, there gradually emerged a people, not very numerous, not very powerful, not very organised, who had a totally new conception of what human life was for, and showed for the first time what the human mind was for."

Athenian democracy was the high point of this innovative culture. It was very different from our own. Citizenship was strictly limited—no women, foreigners, freed men or slaves. So it was a democracy with a certain aristocratic temperament.

And it took shape in the polis—a city-state—that might consist of as few as five thousand and perhaps up to a maximum of fifty thousand citizens. The polis was far more than a patch of land or microstate in the modern sense. The citizens weren't intermittent participants in civic life. To start with, in Athens there was no standing army: in times of war—and there were many of them—each citizen was expected to fight. Each citizen was also expected to serve in public office if asked—and a great number were. This put pressure on everyone to stay well informed and ready to participate. The polis, therefore, represented the whole communal life of the people: political, cultural, moral and economic.

Perhaps the best portrait of this exceptional culture comes from Athens's most famous general and leader, Pericles, who in 430 BC delivered a funeral oration in honor of Athenians who died fighting Persian invaders.

The speech is a tribute to the dead. But it is also a celebration, an explanation and a political idealization of Athenian democracy. Pericles describes for his own and future generations the culture, the tenor and the values of his city.

Pericles begins by explaining that Athens is an innovator, setting a pattern for others. Athens is free and open, all citizens are equal under the law, and anyone may advance by merit. Public life and private life are each valuable and free trade brings in new goods from all around the world. Beauty, art, education and culture adorn the life of the polis. Poverty and obscurity are no shame as long as a citizen makes himself useful. Athenians are generous and openhanded with their neighbors, Pericles explains, not from some small-minded calculation of benefit, but from the confidence of a free and unchained culture. Unlike the Spartans, the Athenians don't spend their time obsessively preparing for war. But Athenians are ready to plan intelligently and act audaciously when necessary. And they have shown themselves to be remarkable warriors.

As part of his word portrait of the polis, Pericles also talks about manners. He explains that in Athens people don't monitor and envy their neighbors, they respect each person's privacy and right to do as he pleases, even when what he does is disagreeable. But this does not encourage lawlessness because an Athenian does not limit himself to observing the written law. The general approbation of his peers is important to him, and to transgress unwritten cultural codes is to risk public disesteem. And, Pericles says pointedly, unlike other nations, in Athens the man who takes no part in his public duties is not considered quiet or unambitious but, rather, *useless.*

This is a democracy in which each person matters, and in which individual acts, great and small, are seen to contribute materially to the culture. It is a community in which each citizen judges his own happiness in large measure by the quality and extent of his social engagement.

It is clear from Pericles that the Greeks were passionately interested in the formation and maintenance of a civil society, but they were just as fascinated by what it means to be an individual and how to construct a good life. Their achievements in science and art, philosophy and drama, sport and spectacle were all associated with this twin intellectual quest.

Happiness (*eudaimonia*), thought the Greeks, was not a passive state but rather an activity. *Arête*, the term usually translated as virtue, more fully means excellent or outstanding. In the Greek mind, happiness meant the act of living in accord with excellence. And the Greeks understood just how hard that goal was to achieve, which is why life for the Greeks was comic and tragic and heroic, all at the same time.

One of the greatest minds to emerge from Athenian democracy was Aristotle's. Aristotle was many things: empiricist, scientist, logician, rhetorician and philosopher. He was certainly no unalloyed democrat; he had his doubts about the merits of rule by the people. He was also an ethicist and the core of his views are laid out in his portrait of an ideal man in *Nicomachean Ethics*.

Aristotle's ideal citizen is very clearly a product of the sort of Athens that Pericles describes. He is, in total, great-souled.

He is prudent, brave, open-minded, reasonable. He is just. He is truthful, witty and good-tempered. He is generous and civilized. Friendship is very important to him. These are his virtues. And, as you might expect, humility and compassion and guilt are nowhere listed as desirable attributes—these are Christian virtues, not Greek ones.

These qualities seem in some respects very modern. The ideal Greek individual has an air of confidence that would inspire even the most dedicated self-esteem addict. And, as in our own era, the Greeks adored and celebrated individual excellence. They had a vivid celebrity culture, in which heroic warriors and beautiful young male athletes were rewarded for their prowess with prizes and laurels and odes and sculptures and vase paintings.

But there is an important distinction between the Greek individual and modern democratic man. Pericles points it out. And Aristotle makes this clear: he believed that man was essentially a political animal, or as Kitto puts it more accurately, "Man is an animal whose characteristic it is to live in the polis." Aristotle believed that society preceded the individual. And what's more, that no citizen could fully express or fulfill his humanity except through society. While Pericles and Aristotle would have differed on many things, on this point they would have agreed utterly.

Tocqueville found and prefigured our modern world of

social disconnection, in which social competitiveness and self-ish individualism draw people apart. Sometimes I fear we have locked ourselves into a foolish and ultimately doomed quest for personal advancement at the expense of the overall well-being of our society and ultimately, therefore, our own. I don't wonder that there is an epidemic of depression in wealthy countries—I am surprised there isn't more of it. When each one of us struggles to win at the expense of others, we will guarantee we all lose.

But the Greek attitude offers another model, in which we acknowledge the bonds linking us as citizens to each other and to our society. Of course we can't, today, have everyone participating personally in politics and government. Our societies are too big and too complex. We need to delegate our citizenship at least in part to a professional political class, advised by skilled and expert public servants.

But we can still have manners—a small, tangible and practical expression of our civic values. We can still enact our citizenship through them every day.

I think my favorite of all the Greek political innovations is the practice of ostracism. When the Assembly decided upon it, each citizen was invited to write upon a piece of broken earthenware the name of any citizen—anyone at all—whom he would like honorably removed from the city for ten years. No need to give a reason. Goodbye. See you in ten. It was a clever way to resolve a political bottleneck or remove the leader of a dangerous faction. But the point is, exile was agony for an Athenian. Nothing was worse than being separated from the society of which you were an integral part—and which was an integral part of you. After all, it was contributing to your society that helped you fulfill your human potential.

And even though we're not Greeks, when we choose to exile ourselves, even metaphorically, from our own society, we also exile ourselves from an important aspect of our own humanity. To put it another way, to connect to our community is to dignify ourselves.

And here is the funniest thing. As I was reading about Athens and trying to imagine what it must have felt like to be a citizen in those great days, I kept feeling a niggling sensation at the back of my head. As if I had a memory of this exuberant world, just below the surface; a sort of deep knowledge that I couldn't explain.

Then one night I remembered, and I laughed out loud. Once, in Sydney, Australia, we *were* Athens in 400 BC. It was, of course, when we hosted the Olympic Games in the year 2000. We created, for a brief and shining two weeks, a polis in the Hellenic tradition, with the world's greatest athletes contesting for athletic arête, and all our citizens uniting to make our city a global beacon of affability and goodwill. The city was scrubbed and clean. Public transport was efficient, and absolutely everyone used it. Most people had some connection with the great event: many thousands volunteered, others paid to go to events or else gathered at sites around the city where large screens were set up. I have never, before or since, smiled with so many strangers.

For once, we were all proud citizens of our polis, subscribing enthusiastically to the greater good. We discovered unexpected personal fulfillment in communal engagement. And there was a veritable epidemic of good manners.

4

Because sovereignty demands self-sovereignty

ONE OF THE DOWNSIDES of manners is undoubtedly that they impose constraints upon our personal freedoms. Rules, etiquette, social taboos—surely they interfere with the free and autonomous exercise of our personhood? Yes, as it happens, they do.

And in our modern era, this is regarded as a very serious drawback indeed because freedom is the twenty-first century's catchphrase and cure-all. It's the dream of every teenager under curfew. It's the hope of every Saturday morning lottery entrant with a mountain of personal debt. It's the slogan of the United States of America as it *liberates* nations from the yoke of dictatorships.

Freedom is beautiful, but it is not the only value. A completely free society would be—is—a recipe for anarchy. Order is surely just as vital: personal security backed up by strong institutions and enforceable rules. Only within agreed-upon structures and limitations can freedom be safely enjoyed.

Manners are some of the limitations society imposes to prevent one person's rights from infringing upon another's. Sovereignty requires self-sovereignty.

Or, as Sigmund Freud put it more psychologically in 1930: "It is impossible to ignore the extent to which civilisation is built upon renunciation, the degree to which the existence of civilisation presupposes the non-gratification (suppression, repression or something else?) of powerful instinctual energies."

Ah, repression. So sadly undervalued in modern life.

Some years ago I worked for an Australian deputy prime minister who had formerly been Australia's minister for defence. Despite his appointment as minister for finance, the minister retained strong and affectionate links with the Australian military, an institution that he greatly cared about and admired. So he was regularly invited to attend military occasions and to give speeches.

The first time I had a close encounter with the Australian Defence Force was when the minister was asked to address the Australian Defence Force Academy, which is a sort of finishing school for the elite Australian officer class. I recall feeling slightly guilty and disreputable, and my spiky days in the eighties marching loudly for nuclear disarmament and the eviction of U.S. military bases in Australia came to my mind as I passed through its portals with my minister for a preliminary cup of tea.

To say I was surprised by the experience is an understatement. As we went to the commanding officer's rooms, it was as if I had stepped back in time to the Edwardian tearoom described in one of my borrowed etiquette books. A silver teapot so polished it caught the light. Fine porcelain teacups. A seat pulled out for me, and pushed in behind. An air of respectful, indeed graceful, charm. I felt myself sitting a little taller, as if the elegant deportment of the officers were infectious. I felt myself pulling my feet under the chair, to hide my scuffed pumps. I wished I had smoother hair. But the courtesies were so refined that I quickly forgot my own inadequacies. The tea was excellent; the conversation stimulating; under such tender ministrations, I was charming, too. Like the minister, I came to realize that there were few things more enjoyable than afternoon tea with trained killers.

I also came to realize that the elaborate and indeed old-fashioned manners of the officer class serve a very important purpose. They are part of the overall code of self-discipline and regimentation that is essential to the effective running of any military. It is part of a code of behavior wisely imposed on them to stop them turning their guns upon each other—or mounting a coup. But it is more than this. When English aesthete and conscientious objector Lytton Strachey was asked during World War I why he wasn't with the troops fighting for civilization, he replied superbly: "But Madam, I am the civilisation for which they are fighting."

We delegate to our military very extraordinary powers. We ask them to make wise judgments that will ensure our safety and preserve our national honor. That's why every day in a democracy the officer class needs to prove to itself and to the wider community not only that its soldiers are fighting for civilization—but more than this, that they, too, are part of the civilization they are fighting for. Their fine manners are a way to demonstrate that they are worthy of this trust.

Of course, fine manners do not automatically lead to goodness. The Nazis were particularly popular with elements of the English aristocracy because their military leaders had superlative manners. Manners are no guarantee against barbarism.

But they do prove that the officer class understands the standard of civilization expected of it by society. If it fails against that standard, then it can be held knowingly accountable.

We give our military so much freedom because we ask and trust them to delimit their actions. Manners are both an instrument to achieve, and evidence of, their self-control.

✤

One night in 1695, a tremor ran through the richest court in the world. At the French palace of Versailles, presided over by the Sun King himself, Louis XIV, an event occurred of such awesome magnitude that the duc de Saint-Simon scurried back to his rooms and wrote that the courtiers were scared to death by what they had witnessed. As word spread of the event, even people who weren't present were reported to have experienced terrors.

The cause of this earthquake? The source of this shock and fear? Quite simply this: the most powerful man in the world had lost his temper.

The story goes as follows. The king had finished his dinner and risen from the table. His hat and cane were handed to him and he made to leave. But suddenly he observed a footman furtively pocketing a sweet biscuit. At that moment, as Saint-Simon said, his "royal dignity forgotten," the king rushed across the room, abused the miscreant and whacked him with his light bamboo cane, which immediately broke on the footman's shoulders. The footman was shocked and ran from the room.

That's it. That's the sum total of the event that reverberated around a terrified court. The royal lapse of manners was considered so appalling that Saint-Simon could not help but seek extenuating circumstances for the king's actions. It turned out that the king had received personally devastating news from the northern front. His illegitimate son, the duc du Maine, had been cowardly and ineffective in battle and therefore the cause of terrible military reverses for the French army. While the military commander and courtiers were covering up this story to protect the king's feelings, no one had told the plan of deceit to the king's plainspoken bath attendant, who reported the humiliating truth to his sovereign.

But while this certainly explained the king's actions, it did not, as far as Saint-Simon and the other courtiers were concerned, in any way justify them. Indeed, the king himself took the view that his failure to control and repress his feelings was a crime. After the incident, he immediately went first to see his saintly wife and then to see his confessor, père François d'Aix de la Chaise, from whom he sought God's forgiveness for his sin.

Manners were critically important to Louis XIV. As a young boy, he had a terrifying experience when a group of nobles mounted an uprising against the crown. So as an adult, Louis XIV decided to centralize power and exert total control over the aristocracy. He built a magnificent home at Versailles and instructed all his courtiers to come and live with him rather than on their estates where they might develop separate power bases and plot against him. To make Versailles attractive, he commissioned a nonstop parade of entertainments—Molière's plays and Lully's music, extravagant masked winter balls, gilded pleasure boats floating down long summer canals, hunting, gambling, summer feasting in the light of sparkling fountains and glorious fireworks displays. And to cap this exercise in domination, the king instituted a system of etiquette so rigorous that simply getting through each day at court became a full-time job.

Pleasure has never been better organized, nor put to such powerful political purpose.

And the severity behind the soft codes was well understood. If any independent-minded courtier absented himself, tiptoeing off to the freedom of his estate or sneaking out to the wanton delights of Paris, the king was bound to notice. Even in a room of three hundred people, the king was famous for spotting a truancy. The phrase people most dreaded was the monarch's quiet "I do not see him," which converted almost instantly into the loss of privileges, favors and financially lucrative appointments.

If the king cannot see you, you no longer exist.

Over the course of Louis XIV's long reign, as the court aged and the glamour wore off, the etiquette became excruciating in its detail and dreary in its execution. People were reduced to agonizing over what kind of chair or stool one was permitted to sit on in the king's presence (if a seat were permitted at all); who had the fortune to receive the small notation (*pour,* meaning for) on his bedroom door that marked the king's favor; and who was privileged to hold a candle at the king's bedtime. The ennui became so extreme that the king's sister-in-law prayed not to have the honor of sitting next to the king at church, because His Majesty would prod her with his elbow to keep her awake. Even the king himself was eventually bored. "What a torture," said his second wife, Madame de Maintenon, "to be obliged to amuse a man who is unamusable."

The curious thing about this world of ceremony is that no one was more bound by it than Louis XIV himself. He lived his entire life in public. Each step in his day had arcane ceremonials attached. Just getting up and dressed in the morning represented an epic ritual. In the morning, a hundred courtiers had the privilege of attending the king's *grand lever.* One gentleman was appointed to drape the dressing gown around the king, another assisted him to adjust the right sleeve and a third to adjust his left. Someone else would have the honor of rubbing the king with orange water and spirits of wine. And so it went on, interminably.

Louis XIV never said, as rumored, *"l'état, c'est moi."* It was redundant. It was perfectly well understood that in Louis XIV, the body personal embodied the body politic. But that did not give him license to behave as he pleased. On the contrary, the king's right to rule his kingdom relied upon his ability to rule himself. As it happened, whacking his footman did not bring about the downfall of Louis XIV's government, and he retained his title as the most powerful king in Europe until his death in 1715. But in order to rule this world, he had to rule himself. That's why his one little slip had the reverberations of a small earthquake.

⚜

Just recently, I was woken from fitful sleep at 7 A.M. by the sound of a cleaner waving a noisy leaf blower around the parking lot of a building across the road from my apartment. This was very annoying, but I soon became aware that the strong southerly breeze was in. That the leaf blower was noisy was bad enough; that it was almost certainly ineffective was intolerable. I became itchy and agitated at the very idea. I found that I very much wanted to shout abuse at someone; I was absolutely ready to lose all self-control.

I knew the signs, of course. I'd been there before, complete with the requisite rationalizations. Damn it, I'm going to go for it, to hell with the consequences. It's what I really think. Why shouldn't I just say it? And I've felt the tingling electric surge you get when you're about to crash through the polite social barricades, when the atmosphere momentarily changes like the air pressure dropping before a tropical storm, when the atoms shift and reassemble around you. And then—that brief intoxicating whirlwind as just for once, hotheaded, you say what you truly want to say.

(Which would be something along the lines of: "What the FUCK do you think you are doing? Do you realize how noisy and POINTLESS that thing is? Haven't you noticed there is a gale force wind blowing? And that all you are doing is creating chaos? Are you a TOTAL FOOL?")

Lucky for me, I didn't say any of it. I can't claim that my manners saved me; my intentions were thoroughly malign. It's just that my inherent laziness and addiction to routine, plus a dash of cowardice, sufficiently delayed action. By the time I had dressed, drunk a cup of coffee and scanned a newspaper, the noise had finished and the moment of blinding fury had passed. I was grateful for the hiatus because later I rang the office manager and was able to explain the problem in a relatively calm voice. This met with a positive response and a productive discussion. While I would have ideally liked to hear that brooms and dustpans were thenceforth back in fashion, instead a compromise was reached that leaf blowers would not commence in the parking lot before 8 A.M.

It might have been exhilarating to deliver the outraged blast. But then again, it might have been nothing more than a momentary self-indulgence to be followed, as night follows day, by 3 A.M. self-disgust and bitter recriminations. Manners always provide the automatic, the healthy, the kindly, the later-to-be-welcomed restraint. They make it possible to re-sume the conversation. They allow for the possibility of a civilized exchange of views rather than a childish airing of sentiment. They allow for the fact that what you think first thing in the grumpy and uncaffeinated morning may not be quite the same as what you think an hour later.

I am glad I did not give in to my base instincts because I almost certainly achieved a better outcome using good manners than if I had succumbed to my first impulse: a naked and raging Lucinda confronting a handyman peacefully waving his, um, tool.

. . . order is necessary to freedom

Louis XIV found that manners are a way to reinforce order. But manners, in a delightful reversal of expectation, can also nurture freedom. If, in the eighteenth century, you had been a brilliant and progressive intellectual; if you had wanted to explore new frontiers in literature, science, art and politics; if you had wanted to create a liberated, enlightened world, there was only one place for you to go. While Versailles was still the center of power for those who were clinging to the past, nearby there was another center of power for those who were inventing the future: the salons of Paris.

A salon was, quite simply, a gathering of guests under

the auspices of an elegant society lady. A core group would convene once or twice weekly and their numbers would be augmented by various visitors and foreigners. The hostess would act as moderator, chair, mediator and facilitator. She would use her charm, discretion, intimacy, tact and personal authority to guide, shape and manage the conversation. In the salons of Paris, women created the premier school of manners in Western civilization.

The salons began in the early seventeenth century with a deliberate emphasis on changing social culture. Women were sick of the violent habits of their men. So they changed the rules. Instead of having duels outside with swords, the men were encouraged to bring their disputes into gilded drawing rooms where conflicts were resolved by words. Just as cutting as the blade, but rarely with mortal consequences. Many of these innovations were incorporated into the early life of Versailles by Louis XIV.

And many of the words we use to delineate the specifics of manners today still echo the culture of these French drawing rooms: *étiquette; savoir-faire; faux pas; bon mot; RSVP (répondez s'il vous plaît)*. Some of the terms are deliciously subtle, like *mauvaise honte*, which means false shame, an emotion that I am fairly sure no longer exists: when your society no longer has shame, there's little incentive to fake it. Or *amour propre*, the bubble of self-regard, most tellingly felt when someone has punctured it. Or *l'esprit de l'escalier*, when you think of something devastatingly witty to say to someone, just that infuriating fractional second after the moment has passed.

And while English is now the global language, French still holds an important place in international diplomacy. The evolution from drawing room manners to international diplomacy makes eminent sense: why go to war when you can sort out differences via discussion, negotiation, mediation and agreement between your appointed representatives? The United Nations and the diplomatic corps still use many French words like *envoy, chargé d'affaires, démarche, aide-mémoire, agrément, rapporteur* and *rapprochement.* Although without, necessarily, the same effectiveness as the *salonnières* in their heyday.

For by the eighteenth century, the salons were so important that the Enlightenment basically took place under the guidance of a few very smart, very alert older French women. And it was a school of tough love: if a salon hostess accompanied you to the door, you knew straightaway that you had failed to please and *you were not welcome again.*

The highly mannered environment of the salons did not hinder the new era of free intellectual discourse; in fact it made it possible. The salon became a space where challenging, controversial concepts could be aired, refined, contested and disseminated. Newtonian cosmology? The demerits of monarchies? The composition of gunpowder? The follies of romantic love? No matter how risqué the subject, the salon was the only place to explore it.

A paradox: the salon was one of the more repressive, contrived institutions in human history. And that's why it played a vital role in the Enlightenment, one of humankind's greatest phases of intellectual liberation.

Baron de Montesquieu spent twenty years thinking about politics and society and contemplating the British political model before he published *The Spirit of the Laws*. This groundbreaking work on government argued for the separation of powers into executive, legislative and judiciary branches so that no single branch could threaten the freedom of the people. These ideas were so politically explosive that the book had to be published secretly. But the salon hostesses of Paris made sure it was a major success, and the Americans went on to use the work as a template for the United States Constitution.

Madame Geoffrin hosted her gatherings on Wednesdays, centering around a young generation of philosophes. They, too, had a daring and dangerous project under way. The *Encyclopédie*. It was a huge undertaking—twenty-one volumes of text and eleven volumes of engravings appeared spasmodically over twenty long, hard years. This tome included everything from how to grow and cook asparagus to the latest theories of inoculation. All the new scientific discoveries were included, as well as technical information on everything from silk-weaving to metal-pressing.

Today this sounds commonplace but then it was extraordinarily dangerous. It was threatening to the governing classes sitting in Versailles because it took for granted religious tolerance, freedom of thought and the value of science and industry. It proposed to take information out of the hands of an elite few and equip ordinary people with the tools to create the future. Revolutionary idea. All the greats contributed to this enormous exercise, including Montesquieu and also Voltaire, Buffon the naturalist and a succession of scientists, technicians and thinkers.

The editor of the *Encyclopédie*, Denis Diderot, wasn't a natural salon guest. He was bold and outspoken. He lacked the social graces. "A great man," remarked Voltaire after meeting him, "but nature has refused him an essential talent: that of dialogue." In the salons this was, of course, a disaster. Madame Geoffrin certainly never allowed heated discussions. She was willing that the philosophers should remodel the world, said one of her critics, on condition that the kingdom of Diderot should come without disorder or confusion. When the conversation became too vociferous, she silenced her guests with her catchphrase: *"Voilà qui est bien,"* she'd say. That's quite enough.

Today this kind of behavior—a bossy woman directing

the conversation—would perhaps be considered socially unacceptable. In our egalitarian times, how dare anyone seek to take social charge? But the salon hostess expected deference and she got it. She controlled the guests, the topics, the time, the style. The salons were so restrictive that even the writing style of the philosophers was influenced by them. As Diderot said, "Women accustom us to making even the driest and thorniest of subjects clear and entertaining since we are always addressing ourselves to them. We gradually acquire a certain facility of expression that passes from our conversation into our style of writing." Through learning to write in the lucid, persuasive style that appealed to the salon set, the philosophers were also learning to write for, educate and eventually politicize the broader public.

By enforcing standards—in conversational style, in writing style, in manners—the women of the salons were effectively creating a neutral, safe territory upon which the most diverse and daring ideas could be safely discussed. They created a common ground for dialogue, making it possible to bring together individuals holding very diverse and even antagonistic views of the world. Out of manners came intellectual emancipation, the prelude to political change. Manners in this context were not about conformity, not at all. On the contrary, they were simply a means to help very different people exchange ideas with one another. Using manners to create the rules of engagement meant that you could debate contested ideas with someone instead of killing them.

In the salons of Paris, manners may have contracted the egoistic individual self, but they expanded the polity. Manners provided the confinement to give birth to freedom.

. . . and manners reconcile liberty to stability

Growing up in the 1960s and '70s, we children minded our manners. At home we said *please* and *thank you*, we did our household jobs, we waited our turn and we knew our place. School was a long, acculturating process of discipline and habit.

But in a curious way, the boring and predictable regimentation of an ordinary childhood protected our privacy and unleashed our inner lives. People always seem to be poking into children's minds these days, encouraging them to express themselves. But a child is often not ready to express. Children need time to absorb, to soak the world in, to dream. I always discovered a creative feeling in myself when I was unoccupied; it was the signal to make something up. If anything, the secret self, the self as yet unknown, could develop in free quietude, in the peacefulness of routine.

And in the meantime I was learning how to live in a society. When we caught the bus or train, we stood up for all adults. This expectation was rigorously enforced. If we did not do so, the adult commuters would not hesitate to berate us, or even ring the school, and then we'd be in dreadful trouble. I remember sometimes feeling resentful, feeling little and weak and tired, with my big schoolbag and weary legs on a long bus ride. But I also knew I was part of a larger continuity, of community. I assumed that one day the young people would stand for me.

No one ever talked to us about freedom. No one ever talked to us about our rights and liberties. On the contrary, we were trained to respect the rights and liberties of others. And of course, the self-respect was deeply implied: this is how worthwhile people behave.

The priests and nuns of our Catholic schools drilled us, quite literally, into order. Weekly marching practice was about taming our individual selves, putting us into sturdy lockstep, and as we wheeled and spun in long even rows, as we sometimes grabbed the chance to step out of line, we always knew we'd have to step back in. And there was a consoling force in this knowledge.

A defined world, a world of contours and shapes and boundaries, is not such a bad thing. "Self-control at least develops a self," said cultural historian Jacques Barzun.

Our ability to control ourselves—or perhaps more accurately, to tolerate controls—is important, because where Louis XIV embodied the state in a single person, the fundamental principle of our modern democracies is that we embody the state collectively. *L'état, c'est nous.* Each one of us carries within us a kernel of sovereignty. And so we each must carry a measure of responsibility, too.

As individuals and as societies, we tread a delicate balance between order and freedom, personal liberty and social stability. Manners are a modest and effective means to help us resolve this complex equation.

And not just to preserve the status quo—but to help us forge a more enlightened future, as well.

5

Because who else can
we call on?

Not so very long ago, we had a group of people in society who carried the banner for manners. We knew them by various names, many of which were not altogether complimentary: the toffs, the nobs, the blue bloods, the grandees, the snobs, the swells, the aristocrats, the upper classes, the ruling classes. Them as opposed to Us. They were society's leaders and they set the style and standard of living to which the rest of us aspired. Whether we liked it or not, they were the elites, and manners were their business.

It didn't matter that most of the population never actually met or socialized with these Olympian citizens. All we needed to know was that the elites enjoyed a lifestyle worth aspiring to, full of glamour, parties, comforts and fun. Their glittering lives—illustrated in the society pages, reported in the vice-regal columns—provided the carrot and stick for generations of careworn parents struggling to inculcate civilized behavior into their children. Mums would say to their grunting boys: *You'll never get to the governor's table if you eat like that!* Grans would say to their slovenly granddaughters: *You won't get away with grubby hands at the queen's afternoon tea!* Social aspiration was the driving force for the spread and codification of manners.

Of course, it was never the case that manners were solely the preserve of the social elite. Indeed, it may well be debatable whether elites ever had the most desirable manners. But it was certainly the case that elite manners set the broader social tone. In *My Fair Lady*, Eliza Doolittle wants to learn the manners of Professor Higgins's class, not the other way around. And even though Eliza's roguish dad is the most sympathetic character of all, no one asks for tuition in *his* amusing and larcenous working-class manners.

So here we are in modern democratic consumer life without an elite class whose authority we unquestioningly accept. In the absence of aristocrats, which group is in a position to go beyond merely minding their own manners and take on the greater burden of influencing manners across society?

Celebrities might seem likely candidates. They are, after all, the most visibly privileged caste in modern life. Beautiful film actresses, wild rock stars, the latest TV personalities— they gaze down like gods and goddesses from the heights of magazine covers and websites and movie screens and stadium arenas and glittering advertisements. Their every move and pronouncement is recorded and replayed endlessly. But while gullible young girls may be dazzled by them, I don't think celebrities are seen as realistic role models. Indeed, their elite status often depends upon a simulated rebellion against the codes of civilized life rather than conformity to them, and certainly not leadership in maintaining them. Like the deistic pantheon of ancient times, they play a darker role: they enact our dreams and our nightmares. We like our celebrities to be mixed up, romantically troubled, creatively wacky, drugged out, in rehab, in litigation, anointed, betrayed, restored, humiliated, resurrected and pursued like wild creatures through the streets. We don't look to celebrities for guidance; we look to them to learn how *not* to live.

Political leaders might naturally be referred to as a source of manners; they certainly once played such a role. But in modern life politicians can't or won't admit to the responsibilities of being elite because any hint of arrogance in political life is a neat shortcut to electoral death. So instead they pretend to be regular folks. Ordinary. One of the people. Just muddling through. They don't like to use the patrician language of leadership. Instead, they deploy deeply egalitarian phrases such as: *I'm listening. I share your concerns. The government certainly meant well. That matter was never brought to my attention.* If they are smart, they pretend to be dumb. Often they *are* dumb, but they act even dumber. And modern politicians are increasingly less likely to act in the genuine interests of their voters than to represent their opinions, which is not at all the same thing. More often than not, our politicians are not leaders but panderers, hostage to daily opinion polls and focus groups. Perhaps the most important point is simply this: too few people aspire to the life of a modern politician for them to be effective role models.

There's another group. As governments have receded from their highly interventionist role in most modern economies, big corporations have become vast engines of wealth-production, employment and influence. And within these corporations we find a cadre of executives who are amassing enormous fortunes. Riding the market boom, flush with stocks and options, accruing vast multiples of the salaries of their subordinates, this new caste is truly a new elite. Barring some major glitch, their children will be rich and their children's children will also be rich. But I recently read a survey that said that even very wealthy businesspeople choose to describe themselves with astonishing and resolute inaccuracy as *middle class* and *on average incomes*. In other words, they'd rather the rest of us took no notice of them and they are not at all keen to take on a social leadership role.

If we accept that our modern elites can't or won't accept the task of shaping our social attitudes and manners, how do we shape and disseminate modern manners? How do we promulgate courtesy?

. . . rudeness won't make us authentic

But first we must address a problem, because many good people don't accept the premise. They aren't at all sure that manners represent an unmitigated good that should be promulgated.

Which is a shame, because for a very long period of time in Western culture, manners were seen as partners of progress. It was widely accepted that social rules made societies better, happier and more civilized. An interest in manners among the ruling classes developed alongside a love of science, culture, legal reforms, literature and art. Reason and manners sat cheerfully side by side.

But then a new generation of philosophers, led by Jean-Jacques Rousseau, profoundly and permanently rearranged the scale of virtues in the late eighteenth century. A new alliance of values began to emerge. Nature was suddenly better than Culture. Feelings were better than Reason. And Sincerity and Spontaneity were higher, nobler and more moral than cold-blooded, artificial, hypocritical, faking-it, clapped-out old manners. This was Romanticism replacing Classicism and we are all still paying the price: "The worst are full of passionate intensity," said Yeats.

These new ideas coincided tellingly with the publication of a book on manners. Over the course of many years, Lord Chesterfield of England had written a series of letters to his illegitimate son, Philip Stanhope. The letters were never meant to be made public. But after Lord Chesterfield's death in 1773, his intimate missives were issued by a relative. And they caused a huge scandal.

Lord Chesterfield had spent a lot of time in France and his advice is heavily influenced by the French view of the world: it is wise and worldly and sophisticated. It assumes that we all live together in society and that manners enable us to advance our own interests in the world. It treats manners at least in part as a useful tool for material progress. Virginia Woolf described the advice as "urbane, polished, brilliant," as indeed it is.

But Lord Chesterfield's book appeared during a time when society was suddenly suspicious about manners. And one, in particular, of his frank and astute observations gave potent ammunition to the new Romantics:

If you would particularly gain the affection and friendship of particular people, whether men or women, endeavour to find out their predominant excellency, if they have one, and their prevailing weakness, which everybody has: and do justice to the one, and something more than justice to the other. Men have various objects in which they may excel, or at least would be thought to excel; and though they love to hear justice done to them, where they know that they excel, yet they are most and best flattered upon those points where they wish to excel and yet are doubtful whether they do or not.

Aha! Here, in Chesterfield's own words, was the evidence, the proof, the smoking gun of the appalling immorality of manners. Manners weren't about indifferent courtesy at all, but about the calculated manipulation of others for personal gain. They were plainly no ennobling feature of human society; on the contrary, they were perversions of natural human goodness. The case was once and for all summed up by Lord Chesterfield's onetime friend Dr. Johnson, who declared that the advice "preached the morals of a whore and the manners of a dancing master."

Chesterfield's world is certainly full of subtlety and, yes, flattery. It assumes that human beings are various creatures, and that social intercourse is multilayered. In a way, far from demeaning human interactions, his advice lends gravity and interest to it all. Because to succeed in his world you must also be thoughtful, considerate, charming and reasonable. And that's no small task. In fact, the standard of behavior the lord sets for his son is arduous and exacting. Among his injunctions: You must be well educated, self-disciplined and modest. You must study in the morning, acquire no less than three languages, inform yourself about all good things. You must observe social decorum, dress soberly but carefully, use perfect grammar, never talk about yourself, never be a bigot or an eccentric or absentminded or a bore.

Now this seems to me like excellent advice to a young person. Indeed, if only there were more of it. I am even prepared to defend Chesterfield *père*'s seemingly Machiavellian recommendations that his son study the strengths and weaknesses of other people and respond to them accordingly. Is that not an ideal way for a young person to discover a great deal about human nature, and perhaps about himself? Often I think the young need time to work out who they are and what kind of person they want to become. What better way than by carefully observing the drives and motives of others? I have no doubt that Chesterfield never intended his son to turn into some shallow or deceitful chameleon. Certainly Chesterfield himself never did. As he lay dying in 1773, a visitor came into the room. "Give Dayrolles a chair," said the courteous lord, and then expired. It's hard to imagine he expected any social advantage from his dying words.

But by then it was all too late, because the Romantic movement was well under way. And in the Romantic worldview, civilization and its attendant baggage—and most particularly manners—came to be seen as a barrier to the expression of natural and authentic man. With Jean-Jacques Rousseau, the fantasy of the noble savage was born, and we live with the sad consequences today.

When Rousseau wrote his famous *Confessions* in 1770, he boastfully claimed at the outset that it would have no imitator. After all, he no doubt thought, who else but J.-J. Rousseau would be so hungry for notoriety that he would be prepared to expose to the world the most intimate details of his life, including farming his five children out to orphanages, unusual sexual experiences (including his encounter with a Venetian courtesan with a deformed nipple) and urinary problems?

As it turns out, just about everybody. Any day on television we can now see Rousseau's cultural descendants confessing the most gruesome details about their marriages or childhoods or dysfunctional relationships or weight problems. They do so with an air of therapeutic self-satisfaction as if, no matter how gravely they have fouled up their lives, their frankness is a tribute to the healthy connection they have forged with their authentic selves.

But here's the thing: as critics like the historian Paul Johnson have pointed out, Rousseau's claim of authenticity was, in fact, bogus. Rousseau used distortion, exaggeration and selective memory both to misrepresent himself and to avenge himself upon others.

As do his successors today.

There's a horrible new category of reality TV programming like *Big Brother* in which people are locked up together for weeks on end. The drama seems to rely upon placing such stress upon contestants that their codes of civility are progressively broken down. In extremis, each contestant's "authentic" self is revealed, for which they may be punished or rewarded via text message. But these are highly artificial situations and the contestants are explicitly selected on the basis of their narcissism and exhibitionism. As it turns out, you *can* fake authenticity.

Rousseau boasted that he had dispensed himself from the artifice and manipulation of manners. He said, ". . . my sentiments are such that they must not be disguised." He declared he was "rude on principle." He proclaimed: "I have things in my heart which absolve me from being good mannered." I am not sure what those things were.

But it seems to me that Lord Chesterfield's advice almost certainly offers a better path to genuine maturity than Rousseau's agenda of rejecting society in pursuit of some elusive "natural" self.

I just can't see that rudeness makes you real.

. . . manners aren't just the tool of right-wing bigots

And another thing.

Not long ago over dinner at a friend's home, I raised the

topic of manners and asked for his views on the subject. I might as well have grabbed a hot poker and prodded him. With an air of mounting rage, he told me unequivocally that he *loathed* manners. He'd spent his whole life escaping from his *repressed* lower-middle-class family in his *appalling* bourgeois regional town. He had always hated manners and he wasn't about to start complaining about the lack of them now. Manners were a way to create dull, *obedient*, uncritical human beings leading boring *conformist* lives.

At that point I felt I fully understood his views. (*So, I gather you're not too keen on manners?*) But there was more, much more.

Manners made my friend *sick*. They made him think of small-town snobbery and *hypocrisy*, like his gloves-and-hat grandmother with her pseudo-refinements and her bigoted opinions about single mothers. Manners created a *tedious*, stultified, rules-bound society. Manners were for social conservatives who were afraid of change. Manners were about telling other people how to behave. Manners were a way to stop all change, progress or creativity. Manners were just *wrong*.

At least I knew where he stood. His was an updated version of the Romantic antipathy to manners. Plus, he had a point.

Today a whole generation of baby boomers like my friend prides itself on the social reforms that were achieved at least in part through bad manners. People who were young in the

1960s broke through the racist and sexist taboos of their parents to unlock a better world. They grew their hair, massed on the streets, burned their bras, made free love and, by defying the rules of etiquette, exposed the encoded bigotry and small-mindedness of their elders. They threw out tired old protocols and brought in a new era of permissiveness, openness, spontaneity and unconventionality. Anti-manners equaled pro-progress.

And real progress was achieved. Huge political battles were fought and won on behalf of the rights of women and African Americans and indigenous peoples and minority groups. When Rosa Parks refused to give up her seat on a bus to a white man in 1955, she broke the law, and she broke the equally powerful taboo of contemporary Southern manners. Some battles, such as the right to gay marriage, are still being waged, and the push for parity is probably irresistible.

An eloquent reiteration of the suspicious baby-boomer attitude toward manners comes from Michael Hanlon in the August 2004 edition of *Spectator* magazine.

> *The conservatives argue that our society is the most ill-mannered in history. Really? Let's go back to the 1950s, shall we, the so-called golden age of politeness when gentlemen always took off their hats on entering a building, children minded their ps and qs and women were unfamiliar with the ways of the doorhandle. "No blacks, no*

> *Irish," seen on boarding houses and hotels after the first waves of post-*
> *war immigration were affronts to decency and good manners un-*
> *thinkable today. People talked, without shame, about "Jewboys" and*
> *"nignogs" and the wealthy showed their inbreeding by behaving with*
> *grotesque condescension towards the lower orders, a term used with-*
> *out irony well into the last century. . . . Now is good; the future,*
> *barring some calamitous accident, will be better.*

The baby boomers were never on their own, of course, in privileging the dream of a liberated future over a repressive present. The post-Napoleonic generation in France and Germany was intensely Romantic, heavily influenced by Rousseau, with disillusioned young people bucking against their elders and dreaming of the untrammeled exertion of the will. The French writer Stendhal, in his *Memoirs of an Egoist,* raged against the politeness of the upper classes in France and England that "proscribes all energy and grinds it down if by chance it exists. Perfectly polite and perfectly devoid of all energy . . ." The Romantics grew their hair, wore pink waistcoats and espoused the liberation of Greece.

After World War I, another disillusioned generation of Bright Young Things embraced the manners of Modernism. T. S. Eliot wrote poems that reflected the deep disillusion with the older generation that had stolen the lives of so many young men in a pointless war: "In the room the women come and go/Talking of Michelangelo," Eliot wrote bleakly of English social life. "We are the hollow men/We are the stuffed men . . ." The inter-war generation cut their hair (the women, anyway) and championed abstract art and the cause of socialism in Spain.

But it seems to me the anti-manners posture is more than just an intergenerational issue, more than just tomorrow defending itself against yesterday.

Michael Hanlon clearly believes that declaring yourself pro-manners is equivalent to declaring yourself a political conservative. And it remains true that conservative politicians are more likely to defend manners than socially progressive ones. This means that when someone in public life asserts the importance of manners, a whole generation of baby boomers instinctively questions their motives. Like Hanlon, in fact, they immediately tag a defender of manners as (a) authoritarian and (b) nostalgic for a bigoted past.

Such labeling makes things awkward for someone like me who considers herself socially progressive but who cares about manners. Is this crossing over to the dark side: aligning oneself with abhorrently bourgeois values; stamping oneself as a defender of the old discriminatory racial, class and gender hierarchies; declaring oneself a relic and a reactionary? Let's face it, who among us wants to be the lead fogy, the head

fuddy-duddy, the number one busybody, the annoying, interfering, nosy so-and-so, the oh, God, no, the manners Nazi?

But it seems to me that these clear-cut political demarca-
tion lines may no longer apply.

The progressive approach has always been about creating
a more egalitarian future. In Australia you'll still hear left-
wing political allies greet each other with an only half-ironic
Comrade! And because the left has always favored state interven-
tion, progressive politicians are more inclined to use legislative
instruments like industrial relations and anti-discrimination
laws to bring about a more civil society.

Take what is now called, usually pejoratively, political correctness. At its best, this is a code—sometimes legislated—
of progressive manners. It means you don't offend members of
minority groups through the use of demeaning language or
stereotypes. But it has a very clear downside. At its worst, it becomes a form of censorship over free speech: when people are
too scared to say what they really think for fear of being la-
beled a bigot.

I personally am delighted that it is socially unacceptable to
say *kikes* or *niggers*. And I am quite content that this requires
some people to think privately the ugly opinions they won't
have the courage to say in public. Hypocrisy may be repugnant,
but it is usually preferable to the confident airing of bigoted

opinions. It is, after all, as La Rochefoucauld noted long ago, "the tribute that vice pays to virtue." I am less comfortable with the legislative emphasis of political correctness. Far more effective than the legal sanction is the social one. It's exhilarating to think that community outrage can force radio shock jocks or celebrities or politicians to apologize, or even resign, for vilifying the members of a particular race or social group.

The other day I was on a bus with a friend when we heard behind us vigorous mutterings about the failings of the driver, who happened to be, I imagine, from South Asia. Two little old ladies were in full flight. I turned and saw a tiny ancient thing with her handbag perched on her lap like a shield against foreign invasion as she pursed her lips and summed up the thrust of the exchange: "Well, I suppose I don't mind if they let them in *as long as they learn our manners.*"

My friend bristled. Here was racism plain and simple. Here was another example of that long, dishonorable tradition whereby manners provided an excuse for social exclusion. But I saw it somewhat differently. Perhaps the little old ladies *were* racist. Many people are. Or perhaps they were merely expressing their fear of newcomers and the inevitable changes they would bring. Even so, they had resigned themselves, if reluctantly, to the evolving order. And they had rightly identified the adoption of local manners by the newcomers as a simple concession to make this change more tolerable.

To my mind there is a rather different downside to manners. It's not so much that they provide cover for the bigot or
hypocrite, but that they induce a kind of social silence on
those who might unmask them. I was reminded of this while
watching the film *Borat*, in which a fictional yokel, bigot and
philistine from an imaginary Kazakhstan tours America. In
one scene, Borat turns up at a classic white, pillared, antebel-
lum mansion for a dinner party where he hopes to practice his
newly acquired Southern etiquette. His host and her guests
behave with immaculate charm and courtesy in the Southern
fashion. Borat progressively ramps up his outrages. Politically
incorrect remarks. Ignorance of hygiene. Then toilet antics—
including producing a bag of shit and asking the hostess what
to do with it. At each step in his downward progress, the
Southerners are comically pained prisoners of their etiquette:
you can see their unease as they try to humor their appalling
guest. The strain on their faces is hilarious and upsetting all at
the same time. Finally, a cheerful whore turns up at the front
door and when Borat brings her to the dinner table, the
Southerners abandon all efforts to redeem the barbarian.
They throw him out. But it took some time. They had tolerated Borat's antisocial behavior for way too long because to do
otherwise might have appeared intolerant, ill-mannered and
even—how cruelly ironic—antisocial.

The political agenda behind Borat's comic antics is an

interesting one. Borat's creator, Sacha Baron Cohen, apparently seeks to do two things—to vividly expose those sexists and bigots who would agree with Borat's ugly views, and to condemn the polite but fundamentally immoral passivity that people tend to adopt when confronted by prejudice. But the film shows, perhaps unintentionally, the positive role that manners can play. It reveals that manners *do* tend to keep the lid on most unacceptable behavior. And when pushed, the decent people in the film firmly reject Borat's racist and sexist worldview.

Now, let us travel to the other side of the political spectrum and consider the idea of manners in relation to conservatism. Conservatives by definition favor the past and resist change. Some still, no doubt, look back nostalgically to manners as a way of reinforcing social inequality, which at its ugliest means those great days when the swinish multitudes, the vulgar masses, the hideous hoi polloi, knew their subservient place. But surely conserving the past is not always and necessarily bad. While people may fondly like to imagine history as a series of unbroken advancements, at worst interrupted by the odd hiccup like the Black Death or World War II, the truth is, it can—and has—gone horribly wrong. Go to Granada and see the tinkling fountains and the magnificent gardens and you want to weep for the demise of that glorious Islamic civilization. Go to Athens and see the crumbling architecture of classical Hellas.

Go to Macedonia and see the Byzantine frescoes disappearing into the stone walls like the culture that created them.

No civilization lasts forever, and it is nearly always a close-run thing. If you were a Roman in the fifth century, the barbarians really were at the gate. And when the curtain comes down on a civilization, it can be a very long time before it rises again. Even the basics can be so swiftly forgotten. After the Roman demise, it was centuries before baths came back into fashion: those years weren't called the Dark Ages for nothing.

There's merit in conserving things. Today we try to conserve biodiversity, energy, heritage buildings, remnant bushland. Just as we look to conserve the best of nature or architecture, surely it's worth remembering our most delightful customs?

Manners can never, of course, be permanently fixed like fossils in amber. They must, and do, evolve and adapt. But at their best they are a species of cultural memory. The things we do today—shake hands, clink glasses—become an affectionate nod to our past. A salute to our ancient humanity and to the funny, anxious rituals of our forebears. Men once shook hands to prove they carried no weapons. They clinked drinking vessels to slop wine into each other's glasses, disproving the presence of poison. Today, as we forgetfully play out the rituals of modern life, we are nevertheless communing with the mysterious and delicate process that is our civilization.

To me this seems very beautiful—and perhaps it explains why I find myself so sensitive to the signals that these links are becoming more and more attenuated, why I am so alarmed by the little signs that we are untethering ourselves from our historical moorings.

. . . and they advance social progress

Here's a thought: What if—in our modern era—manners were not conservative but subversive?

What if those old-fashioned conventions and courtesies that take up time, make no money, serve no commercial utility—what if, far from upholding some ugly status quo, they were in fact a protest against it, a green oasis of gentle civilization in the jungle of consumer capitalism? What if the little gestures that make life sweeter and kinder and more predictable were a wonderful rebuke to the cruel consume-work-die routine of modern life? What if manners were, rather like recycling and community volunteering, a modest way to uphold the values of community in the midst of the rampant commercialization of modern life? And what if, instead of repressing our authentic selves, manners allowed them to flower?

In 1928, one of the founding members of the Bloomsbury group, art critic Clive Bell, wrote and published a little book called *Civilization*. He dedicated his essay to his dear friend

Virginia Woolf, with whom he had already discussed many of his ideas on the subject.

Bell was writing in the aftermath of World War I, spurred by the death of millions of young Englishmen who were sent to fight in the trenches for the cause, their government told them, of civilization. Having lost many of his friends in that war, Bell considered it might be worthwhile working out what exactly was this "civilization" in the name of which so many young men had died. Many of the ideas Bell expressed would now be considered old-fashioned and indeed politically incorrect, which is probably why I enjoyed them so much. Bell considered that the first step toward civilization was "the correction of instinct by reason"; the second, "the deliberate rejection of immediate satisfactions with a view to obtaining subtler."

Bell argued that all civilizations depend upon a small but potent core of highly civilized individuals. A leisured class is essential, Bell said. And he explained exactly what this leisured class required: leisure, of course, but also economic freedom and liberty to think, feel and experiment—no doubt a list all too familiar to Virginia Woolf, who agreed that every artist needs a room of her own.

Bell was writing at a time when the British economy was an inflexible, near-broken machine and British society was similarly rigid and restrictive. He assumed that there were only two possible classes: those living comfortably off capital, and those working hard for wages. The fortunate few who had capital were the group from which the leisured class might spring. In his view, almost all forms of moneymaking were detrimental to intense and refined states of mind, because almost all tired the body and blunted the intellect.

But Bell stressed that leisured did not necessarily mean pampered—the Athenian Greeks, as he noted, lived in great simplicity and yet had the finest of all civilizations. And indeed, Bloomsbury itself was noted for the relatively simple lifestyles of its members. And its progressive politics. Think of what came from Bloomsbury—the feminism of Virginia Woolf, the economics of John Maynard Keynes, the sexually liberated lifestyles of nearly all its members and a legacy of intelligent freethinking that has influenced successive generations.

Of course, Bell's basic point is unimpeachable. Civilization has always been a function of time left over after the necessities of food and shelter have been dealt with.

But in modern life it seems to me that the circumstances for civilization are not necessarily the all-or-nothing proposition that Bell imagined. The truth is that many of us do have the opportunity to create lives that are civilized. The world is no longer divided between capitalists whooping it up on the one hand and workers laboring under the yoke on the other.

Most of us in the modern middle class, with our mortgages and retirement funds and jobs, are both capitalists and workers. We have much greater flexibility. We may work full-time for ten years then take a year off, or obtain our long-service leave, or take a study break. We may choose to work part-time. We can move in and out of jobs, we can work as contractors or consultants, we can telecommute, we can shift between companies and job locations. Never in human history have we ordinary people had such capacity to influence our own working lives.

We live and work in very flexible economies. And while this presents its own challenges and anxieties, at least we are not condemned to work in the same dreary office for forty years before getting a gold watch at age sixty and dropping dead a sad year or two later.

And here's another thing. It costs so comparatively little to be civilized in modern life. It takes more money to buy a CD by a venomous rap artist or this week's dreadful pop princess than three Mozart symphonies or a Duke Ellington songbook. It's cheaper to buy any of Robert Fagles's translations of Homer's *Iliad* and *Odyssey*, or a Flaubert, Conrad or Bellow in a bargain bookshop than to buy the latest chick-lit offering at Borders. The Internet has the most extraordinary free resources available. You can tour the world's wonderful museums, read back copies of the *Paris Review* interviews, download full texts of out-of-print books or join in spirited chats with experts devoted to European film history. Sometimes I am quite alarmed at how little civilization costs today; in our relentlessly commercial era, this is a saddening sign of how little it is valued.

The one seriously inhibiting factor, of course, is time. Leisure is in short supply in modern life. The irony is that this problem applies most dramatically to our most affluent citizens. Most senior executives toil such long hours they have no time to enjoy their fortunes. The company operatives a little further down the chain are rather like well-compensated slaves: body and soul available at all times to their corporate masters. The significant financial compensations—flashy cars and in-ground pools and new kitchens—are shiny handcuffs to bind the workers to their income and enforce their fealty.

But some of us are changing. We are stepping back from the path of unbridled economic aspiration. Downshifters, part-timers, urban hermits, sea-changers, tree-changers—call us what you will, but we are gently, genially and sometimes necessarily bailing out. We are climbing off the treadmill.

We are now the ones who enjoy leisure—or leisure enough—to take part in and contribute to civilization. We have internalized the delightful paradox that a lower income might grant to us a higher standard of living. If we are lucky, we have discovered that the redundancy package is modern life's greatest career opportunity. And if multitasking is the enemy of manners, which it is, then a slower, sweeter, simpler life might well be a rich source of manners. With time to think, write, cook, read. We are creating, not lifestyles but life itself.

Of course, for many people the child-raising years will pass by in a necessary blur. They will simply have to juggle all their myriad responsibilities in the messy, sustaining fog of family life. But look at the cultural life of any Western city and you'll see that once their family work is done, many people resume their wider interests. Older men and women are among the most active community volunteers in the soup kitchens and visiting the frail elderly. Women, in particular, are the patrons of the arts, the enthusiasts at writers' festivals, the prime movers at book clubs and library meetings.

Those of us who have stepped back find we can contribute to civility in all kinds of small or large ways. We don't add to the stress and traffic jams of rush hour. We are off-peak users of energy and water. We take up fewer resources than people inhabiting high-rise, air-conditioned office buildings. When I worked in government and business, I was always rewarding myself for my labor. Now I don't need to spend anything like the same amount of pep-me-up money on expensive shoes and handbags to console myself for all those weekends lost to work. Less shopping, less rubbish. Some of us have the time and energy to collect our neighbor's mail, or talk to the community board about the new arrangements for the local park, or contribute to the co-op board in our block of apartments or make a casserole for a sick friend, or even just to invite someone stressed and busier than we are to go ahead of us in the supermarket queue.

None of these measures are about being a more virtuous person. They are a delightful by-product of time and choice. In fact, it's a privilege to live like this. It's much easier to be nice when you are happy. And being nice makes you feel good.

Clive Bell thought that to be truly civilized you had to be part of the leisured class continuously and from early life. Perhaps our era is different. Perhaps we can draw down on— and contribute to—our civilization with differing intensities, according to the different phases of our lives. And our later years might be some of our most fruitful.

A final thought. The night that my friend told me he loathed manners started out quite badly. I recall slumping back in my seat, wondering if his negative views were widespread. Perhaps people of goodwill, people whom I respected, appeared to have given up on what I considered to be a basic and really undeniable condition of civilization. *What hope is there?* I said to myself despondently.

But then: before his little daughter went to bed, my friend quite unself-consciously counseled her to say good night politely to Mummy and Daddy's guests. She came up close to me and told me solemnly that she was allowed ten minutes of bedtime reading before lights out. She had a good book and she hoped to finish it tonight. And then she was lovingly shepherded by her father upstairs.

6

Because McDonald's doesn't own manners

IN MAY 2004, the prime minister of Australia once again reminded Australians that manners are important. He said that we were living in a less civil society than even ten years ago. He asked parents to bring up their kids with regard to the old-fashioned courtesies. And then, perhaps as helpful guidance, he referred to what he saw as a prime source of civility in modern life: fast-food chains. "Some of the friendliest, well-mannered young people are the ones you find at McDonald's," declared the prime minister.

For reasons I can't quite express, I went into a small decline at this statement and took temporarily to my bed. I must have been in a weakened state because the idea of McDonald's as my prime minister's notion of a civilizing Australian institution was just too much to bear.

It's not that he was necessarily all wrong. McDonald's came to Sydney when I was a teenager. And it was a rare business at that time because it was prepared to employ young people, give them a little training and put them to work in a bright and shiny environment. It seemed a lot more fun to many than washing Dad's car or mowing the lawn for pocket money. Although I must snootily admit that I never took to McDonald's cuisine.

When I was first thinking about this essay I assumed, if I can put it this way, that all social interactions are equal. That civility and incivility have the same quality and effect no matter where they are found. But gradually I came to realize that this is not true.

When we interact with people in a commercial sense—when we pay and buy, when we sell and exchange—the parameters change. One party in the transaction has a motive behind his or her courtesy. In such a case, manners are not sublimely indifferent. They are directed to a specific end. The fact is, when young people are polite to their customers at McDonald's, they are being paid for it. Money changes everything. Not necessarily for the better.

When I was growing up there were two categories of salespeople: hearty and surly. But now I have noticed that people trying to sell me things are becoming more and more polite. It's true. You might not have noticed, but they are all trying very hard indeed. Sometimes infuriatingly hard. Even the computerized telephone systems are polite. *Thank you for holding. Your call has been placed in a queue and will be attended to shortly. Meanwhile please enjoy your music program. Please ensure you have your account number ready. Thank you for waiting. Your call has progressed in the queue. If you'd like to purchase our new software, please press four. All our operators are currently busy. Your call has progressed in the queue. Your call is important to us.*

This careful courtesy is not, of course, necessarily co-equivalent to good service. But I am sorry to say that commercial manners do not incline me to be more polite in return. On the contrary, these transactions bring out the very worst in me. Somewhere deep inside I simply don't feel the same respect for manners when I am expected to pay for them. I was thoroughly rude to some poor woman calling from God-knows-where in India, just trying to earn a living selling cell phones. I left her saying, *"Madam! Madam!"* in a pleading tone as I slammed down the phone. Another time, after being put through to three different areas of a computer company, I was finally told that no one there could help me with the breakdown of my machine—that's when I, too, more or less broke down in a welter of abuse. I have been nastily sarcastic via email when some flowers I ordered online for a friend did not arrive. It's only my natural cravenness that has prevented me from being rude to people in shops. And in each instance of my rudeness, the salesperson has not been rude back to me but has stoically—almost heroically—retained a demeanor of courtesy.

Afterward I have always felt terrible. I had intended to send a message to a corporation but I just ended up ruining the working day of a human being.

And yet, despite the legitimate or unwarranted abuse of staff by people like me, the trend toward retail politeness intensifies. It is not only a feature of commercial interactions, it is also and increasingly a theme of modern sales. If you look up the websites of big consumer companies, many will have published the equivalent of etiquette guarantees—customer service charters, customer "bills of rights," "ask once" customer commitments. These are all about assuring customers that they are highly valued and will be treated with courtesy and respect.

A major bank is running a series of TV advertisements proposing its superior courtesy as what the marketing companies call its "unique selling point." In each advertisement an ordinary person is subject to a telling instance of the rudeness of modern life. No one will hold a door open for a man carrying a huge pile of documents. A pregnant lady on the bus is pointedly left to stand up by her complacent co-travelers. Cut to our hero and heroine sighing with delighted relief when they enter a branch of this particular bank. *We won't slam the door in your face! We'll give the pregnant lady a chair!* The bank presents itself to us as a refuge from the incivilities of modern life.

But I fear that this marketing campaign may backfire. Manners in the world of commerce are not a gift, they are a promise of service. And if customers find that the ultimate promise isn't kept, they can get very cross indeed. The finer the manners, the bigger the letdown and the more explosive the response.

True story: In January 2007, *The Sydney Morning Herald* reported on the latest findings about so-called customer rage. Despite the best efforts of so many companies, people were just getting crosser. The findings showed that the trigger times for rage were becoming smaller and smaller. The most serious incidents occurred when there was "a double deviation," that is, when a customer felt that he or she had been treated disrespectfully twice in succession.

- A man who was not allowed to return an unused can of paint drilled a hole in it and carried it dripping around the store.
- A woman who wanted to exchange baby formula at a drugstore became infuriated, returning later to spray the formula over staff.

- A man who was told his electricity would be discon-
nected when his bill was eight weeks overdue threatened to blow up the power company's headquarters.
- A woman whose light mocha was not stirred prop-
erly poured it on the counter.
- A woman was still in tears six months after a department store sold her a faulty air conditioner and refused to replace it.

Yes, I, too, felt that the light mocha incident was an odd in-
clusion in that list. And why shouldn't the electric company
disconnect the power of a persistent defaulter? But if the ex-
amples are not particularly helpful, nevertheless the story
made me wonder if what people were reacting so vehemently
against was not a problem with manners but a problem with
service. To put it bluntly: companies shouldn't imagine they
can woo you with smooth words and smiles and then, having
won your business, treat you like crap. And it must be remembered, it's not just the customers who suffer.

True story: In March 2006, German researchers claimed
that enforced enthusiasm in the workplace was making people
sick. Psychologists at Frankfurt University discovered that
flight attendants, sales personnel, call-center operators and
waiters were professionally required to be nice to people.

They discovered that this fake friendliness was causing depression and stress and even a lowering of the immune system, leading to more serious ailments. As part of the study, test students working in an imaginary call center were subject to abuse from clients. Some of the participants were allowed to answer back; the others had to maintain politeness all the time. The admirably named Professor Zapf noted that every time a person was forced to repress his true feelings, there were negative consequences for his health. Professor Zapf's unstartling conclusion was that we should show more respect to those in the service industries.

Waiters and call-center operators are not called frontline staff for nothing. It must seem like warfare to them as they grapple with the gripes of customers, especially if they are not personally responsible for the customer's dissatisfaction or are not in a position to rectify a problem themselves.

Our lives are governed by commerce. That's the reality. Short of living in a tree in the jungle, we can't escape. Even at home we are bombarded with advertising on our televisions, radios and computers. Sales pamphlets and letters of promotion are stuffed into our mailboxes. Even our bills are regularly accompanied by enticements to purchase other products. The phone rings with unsolicited offers for holiday clubs or credit cards or insurance. And we can't attempt to engage with the culture in the most humble way—go to a movie or a football game or a concert—without pumping music and big-screen advertisements and programs covered with marketing material.

Sometimes I have the creepy sensation that at all times, somehow, somewhere, there's a smiling woman with a headset waiting for my call. It's a feeling of being passively stalked.

So while I would like to agree with the prime minister and argue that the *Have a nice day!* culture at McDonald's genuinely contributes to the formation and maintenance of a civil society, I am not sure it is the case. Of course good manners are always more desirable than rudeness. But the evidence so far is that the fashion for commercial civility is not making more customers any happier—and appears to be making many staff sick.

. . . corporations don't own our souls

Now let's take a peek inside the big and expensive corporations. Here we again find salespeople but this time they sell things for thousands and millions of dollars instead of just the price of a hamburger—and also professionals of all kinds who crunch the numbers, organize human resources, run the supply chain, devise the marketing campaigns, audit the accounts, manage compliance with tax and other laws, design new products and engineer the information technology systems.

Here the atmosphere is a little different.

Last year my friend Aaron graduated from a university with excellent results and started looking for a job as a lawyer. As an older graduate, with a background in community politics, Aaron was eagerly taken up by a prestigious city firm and he conducted a first round of interviews with the associates and partners. Then he received feedback from the recruitment officer to the effect that, while Aaron had all the right professional qualities, he appeared to lack *enthusiasm*. This was something he needed to work on before his final meetings with the senior partners.

Aaron was puzzled by this. He consulted our mutual friend Alice, who had worked for similar companies.

"Let me guess," said Alice. "You said something like, 'I am moderately interested in this job where I propose to utilize my skills and abilities on your behalf, for which you will pay me an appropriate salary.'"

"Pretty much," said Aaron. "What else was I meant to say? Wouldn't anything else sound fake?"

Alice haw-hawed. "Of course! Your job is to offer undying loyalty to the firm; theirs is to declare they'll be loyal to you in return. There is no reason to believe either of you will be speaking the truth."

"So I need to look really excited and say, 'I would *love* to be a regulatory lawyer at your firm and I've dreamed of it for years.'" Aaron blushed at the very idea of such excess.

But Aaron laid it on and got the job. After which he was deposited in an office, handed three hundred pages of documents and left alone for weeks on end. At one point his phone had been silent for so long he called Alice and asked her to ring him at his desk to make sure it was still working. He told her that he could not imagine a job where unbridled enthusiasm would be a less helpful attribute.

Aaron's experience is not uncommon. In the big corporations today it is simply not enough to turn up and do your job. You have to be pumped, you have to be firing, you have to have an edge. It seems they don't just want your body, they want your soul, as well. I do not exaggerate.

A management consultant once boasted to me about the new program his firm was introducing to a top mining company. This was all about engaging and motivating employees and connecting them more closely to the aspirations of the company with, of course, the ultimate goal of increasing productivity and performance. He actually said it was all about "bringing the soul to work." He beamed with pride at the idea. Thinking back, I can't remember whether this was a gaze of pure innocence or unadulterated cynicism—either was possible and both were scary.

And I could have cried. I wanted to say: "It's bad enough for most people to bring their bodies to work. Do you have to have their very souls, as well? And what if they don't want to bring their souls to the office? What if they'd rather leave them resting peacefully at home?" (I wanted to say this, but in fact, struck dumb by horror, I said nothing.)

I've heard of one advertising agency that has *impact* meetings at 7:30 each morning where loud music is blared out to create high energy and the operatives are required loudly and excitedly to shout their sales targets for the day. *Impact.* As if you are in a high-speed car crash, which is exactly what it must feel like. Another company explicitly tells job applicants that their "attitude and enthusiasm" are as important as their experience—as if ten years in marketing is only valuable if you can emote convincingly about it.

Some of the top professional firms, like management consultancies, demand more than just skill, competence and co-operation. They want a total commitment. While my friend Aaron was sent to his own lonely office, more commonly these businesses put their staff in open-plan spaces so that they have no real privacy but must relate to each other almost as intimately as family members. Casual clothing emphasizes an egalitarian mood and a feeling of belonging. Staff are encouraged to form close-knit teams aided by bonding sessions and boot camps and "away" meetings. To add to the sense of an all-embracing and even domestic environment, bright office cafés, time-out stations, food bars and comfy couches are installed, so that there are even fewer excuses for venturing beyond the corporate domain, let alone going home. The importance of the commitment to this ideology of work is reinforced by explicit performance measurements such as "contribution to firm culture," as if the firm were a small nation protecting a precious cultural heritage.

Perhaps it sounds as though this would be an environment in which manners might thrive. Where close collaboration would be actively enabled by courteous modes of interaction. But often this is not the case. Aggression, testosterone, high energy levels and a competitive spirit are valued. Big targets, extravagant demands and grueling timetables are admired. Pressure and speed are celebrated. And if a particular individual is making enough money for the firm, then his or her petulant, virulent and rude behavior will be quite rationally excused on the grounds that he or she is contributing to the overall good of the firm.

There are many companies in which no one wants to talk about manners because they employ too many genuinely effective people who don't have any.

It might validly be argued that all this is a matter for individual businesses, and not really relevant to a discussion of broader civility. Who cares if these high-paying companies demand extreme levels of emotional engagement from the staff? Who cares if bullies and pigs are tolerated in these elite workplaces?

But it does matter, because these organizational cultures don't just exist unto themselves. They are a part of the world we live in and they employ many talented people. The way they operate has an impact on broader civility.

Here I am aboard one of those Friday evening commuter flights. The plane is full of up-and-coming young operatives from IT companies and telecommunications firms and management consulting partnerships, heading home after a week on a project. They are all remarkably similar: uniformly thirtyish, male and prematurely balding. They each carry a laptop and an earpiece. They exude the sour smells of lunch, sweat, a few beers and corporate fear.

Three of us nudge into our row, stow our bags, sit down, strap up. I am in the middle. We're so close, we intermingle elbows, shoulders, breath and knees. We do not look at one another, rather into the middle distance of the headrests in front of us. No one wants to engage. This is almost certainly the nearest any of us have ever come to a threesome. Yet we do not exchange a word.

I lean down to extract a magazine from my handbag. The guy on my right puts the volume of his headphones on so loud I can hear the thrashing bass and my heart and breastbone throb in painful and unwilling chorus. I sit upright and cautiously attempt to turn the slick colored pages without jerking my elbows or spreading my hands too wide, and at the same time the guy on my left throws his head back and immediately begins loudly to snore. He then utters a snort so bone-shatteringly momentous that he wakes himself up. He sits up, sighs loudly, shakes his head for a moment, then carefully places it under my ear and falls back deeply asleep. The man in front of me immediately reclines his seat to the maximum so that my magazine is now pressed up to my nose and the man behind me completes the compression by putting his feet directly into the small of my back.

This is before takeoff.

Pinioned between four men, I reflect on modern life. No one here is deliberately rude, no one is nasty, and yet, to say I feel violated would not be going too far. This is the closest physical contact I have had with any man—men—apart from my husband, for years. I might as well be lying in bed with four strangers, all of whom are ignoring my very existence. This is, to say the least, unflattering. And yet we are all here, now, together. Yes, even you, I think, looking down at the sad depleted follicles of my somnolent traveling companion.

But gradually it occurs to me that these men are weary. Not just bone-weary but soul-weary. They have a sort of emptied-out quality, a telltale post-work flatness. Nothing comes back at me from behind their eyes. And I realize that this airline flight is, in a funny way, a relief, a vacation from affect, a welcome escape from the office and its exhausting, complex and passionate interactions. They simply don't have the stock of emotional energy required to be civil on the plane to a stranger. They can't face the stress of nodding and saying, *Good evening.* They don't want to look at me, in case I try to engage them. They want to ignore me as if I don't exist. More important, they want me to ignore them as if they don't exist, either.

Which is true, in a way. They are utterly hollow. If they have any emotional energy left, they are understandably storing it for their wives and children and the few friends they have outside work. That's when the lights will come on again and the outer life resumes.

At the end of the flight we all clamber out and join the glum stream winding down the corridors and escalators and swivel our heads anxiously as the baggage carousel grinds round and round. We finally disperse and I slump into the taxi queue. I feel rather as though I have had very bad sex—a grimy, well-handled feeling without the afterglow.

I appreciate the dignity of labor. I do. And I am glad that these young men are all keen to be successful and make lots of money because I can then enjoy all the useful and beautiful products and services that will flow from their efforts.

But they are achieving these good things in workplace cultures that exaggerate the value of work and downgrade the importance of civility. They pay a heavy price for this and so do we.

※

Recently, I came across a book called *The No Asshole Rule: Building a Civilized Workplace and Surviving One That Isn't,* written by Robert I. Sutton, a professor of management science and engineering at Stanford University. I came across it not because I routinely scan the business literature, but because it shot immediately to the best-seller list in my favorite bookshop. As Sutton explains, he wrote the book because a short blurb he penned about *assholes* in the *Harvard Business Review* attracted a massive response. I have to explain here that I am going to use his term because, well, it's his. (And it is, of course, incorrect. The correct term is *arseholes.*)

At last! I thought. The book I have been waiting for. A book that will explain that all the hype in the world can't disguise the fact that a company is still just a collection of individuals gathered to achieve certain commercial objectives—and that the fundamental human things still apply.

Sutton lists twelve everyday actions assholes use: personal insults, invading someone's territory, uninvited physical contact, threats and intimidation, sarcasm, abusive emails, status slaps designed to humiliate, public shaming, rude interruptions, two-faced attacks, dirty looks and ignoring people. It seems to me as though every single one of these misbehaviors is, at minimum, a matter of manners.

Sutton goes on to consider the economic costs to firms of these behaviors by bullies and jerks, the way dysfunction can spiral through the office and how companies can make an active decision to create harmonious and productive workplaces.

And reading this I became very excited because I was sure that Sutton would go on to explain why civility in the workplace is important and how it can be created and what can be achieved by it. But in these naive expectations, I couldn't have been more wrong.

In an apparent contradiction of his own agenda, Sutton explicitly says that his book is not about the virtues of manners. Not at all. As he says, he truly believes in the virtues of conflict, the right kind of friction and the merits of vigorous debate. He can't stand spineless people. As far as he is concerned, firms mustn't stifle creativity and populate their corridors with dull clones. "If you want to learn about the virtues of speaking quietly and the nuances of workplace etiquette," Sutton concludes bluntly, "then read something by Miss Manners."

And that's it. Sutton defines manners so narrowly as to justify their exclusion from his thesis. He wants to make civilized workplaces, but doesn't want to accept that civility plays any role in achieving this. He does, however, have many good stories and suggestions about dealing with the dysfunction caused by assholes. Some of them—such as "constructive confrontation" courses—sound to me like fancy terms for teaching people to handle differences using good manners. But Sutton prefers the jargon.

This sensible man from Stanford feels so uncomfortable with the term "manners" that he defines it away as equivalent to spinelessness, lack of creativity and conformity.

. . . and manners are no barrier to greatness

When I was in my early twenties, I went to work in the Australian Department of Foreign Affairs. I thought of myself as young and smart and vibrant—when all I was, was young. When I got together with my new contemporaries, we were scathing of our older (male) supervisors, with their beige suits and their bland courtesies and their infuriating understatements. Bloodless! we thought. Dull! Now I look back on those tepid men with unlikely nostalgia.

One legendary departmental secretary was a tiny colorless egghead of fierce intellect. When a briefing note was returned from his office, there were only four likely responses. If he wrote *Noted*, you were relieved: this was almost always what he wrote. If he wrote *Thank you*, you were very pleased with yourself. If he wrote *Many thanks,* then you went zooming into joyful outer space: he hardly ever wrote *Many thanks.* When he wrote *This needs further thought,* you panicked.

The egghead had no need for hyperbole. No need for the injection of modern exaggeration. Nor had he any need to yell, throw things or respond to incompetence with abuse. The restricted palette of his reactions only served to intensify the effect of his communications. Everyone knew what he meant and where they stood.

The egghead would never have been deluded into thinking that an idea presented in a loud and intimidating voice was better than one presented quietly. Nor that a personal attack was more effective at modifying employee behavior than a clear and succinct reproof related to the professional issue at hand. He would have supposed there was a time and place for the spontaneous emotional response, but he himself had never happened to come across such a time and place. Ideas were debated, but not in dramatic shouting matches filled with the frisson of testosterone and tension. More usually in a low-key conversation, carefully guided by the chair of a meeting, based on well-prepared notes and followed up by a brief clarifying minute.

It is bizarre and wrong to imagine that manners in the workplace are a cork in the fizzing bottle of creativity, or a roadblock on the pathway to achievement. Equally, of course, they are no guarantee of competence or a ticket to glory. But they can certainly help.

One of history's greatest statesmen and bureaucrats was the eighteenth-century French foreign minister le duc de Talleyrand. He never left home without white pancake makeup, a wig and an elegant limp (clip-*clop*, clip-*clop*). His exquisite, icy cold manners and ruthless decision-making frightened people: some made the sign of the cross when he walked by to ward off the devil, which was particularly ironic given that he had once been a bishop. Talleyrand's menacing authority was intensified by his air of boredom, his famed pauses, his lassitude and his undying commitment to a long chat with his chef every morning about the menu for dinner.

And there was professional method in this refined and lethargic approach. Talleyrand was so brilliant, his acumen so renowned, his judgment so astute, he served in the successive and utterly oppositional governments of the ancien régime, the Revolution, Napoleon and even the restored Bourbon monarchy. In the history of political survivors, Talleyrand must rank among the greatest.

In his biography of Talleyrand, the Englishman and diplomat Duff Cooper lauded Talleyrand's greatest professional attribute. Cooper noted admiringly:

He discouraged excessive zeal even in his subordinates, and when he relinquished the Ministry for Foreign Affairs, he said, presenting the permanent officials to his successor, "You will find them loyal, intelligent, accurate and punctual, but, thanks to my training, not at all zealous." As M. de Champagny evinced some surprise, he continued, affecting a most serious manner, "Yes, except for a few of the junior clerks, who, I am afraid, close up their envelopes with a certain amount of precipitation, every one here maintains the greatest calm; hurry and bustle are unknown."

As Talleyrand understood, manners permit you to start small and slow. To say: *I'm sorry to hear that.* And: *Events are under review.* And: *It appears to be quite serious.* To keep things formal and calm and quiet. And the pause, the time, the slowness are an aid to truth and to good judgment as much as to style. Talleyrand's famous maxim? *Surtout, pas de zèle:* Above all, no zeal. Cooper explained that this deliberate manner of conducting business was of particular service to Napoleon, who, though he loathed the effete Talleyrand, recognized his admirable foreign policy skills. Napoleon was often glad to find that instructions he had given with too little consideration had not been acted upon several days later when he was already prepared to cancel them.

And it's not as if Talleyrand was never placed under

duress. Throughout his career, he was threatened by some of the greatest challenges any statesman in history has had to face, as France reeled from revolution to war to empire and counterrevolution. He had to have his wits about him at all times. Indeed, he was necessarily a master of duplicity, calculation and thoughtful corruption. And he had his own codes of honor. As far as he was concerned, the governments he served were merely temporary institutions, while the interests of France remained permanent. And it was these interests he served. As well, of course, as his own.

Napoleon, once driven to fury when he heard of Talleyrand's latest plotting, hurled public abuse at his foreign minister, ending with the famous attack, "You are just shit in a silk stocking!" People were shocked, of course. And they naturally assumed this meant the end, finally, at last, of the everlasting Talleyrand. So there was a murmur of amazement when Talleyrand appeared at the next grand ball, utterly unperturbed, and bowed low to kiss Napoleon's hand. Far from seeing this act as one of pathetic subservience, everyone knew this meant that Talleyrand was in fact capable of anything. Napoleon retained Talleyrand's shitful but essential services. And Talleyrand, of course, outlasted Napoleon.

If manners can be of value when the highest national interests are at stake, surely they can't hurt in the design, marketing and sales of the latest high-tech product?

✢

I was disappointed with the *No Asshole* book, but I think it has merit as an advance in the discussion. Even if Sutton disdains manners, manners are what he is really talking about. And plenty of organizations now accept that they can be successful without draining the lifeblood from their employees. These companies are trying to improve working conditions for their staff. Some are putting anti-bullying measures in place to stop the worst offenders against manners in the workplace. And perhaps if they do this, the benefits will flow through to all those stressed-out frontline workers, who then won't have to feel as though they are sandwiched between abuse by their customers and mistreatment by their employers.

And I have made a small resolution. As recommended by Professor Zapf, I am going to try very hard to be polite to people with whom I am having a commercial conversation, no matter how hard this may be. And, on those rare occasions when I come across higher-end operatives away from the office, I am going to be kind to them, too, because they are also part of our polity. And because one day, who knows, they may well return to the world and need to know how to be part of it. Those exhausted businessmen may well be the next generation of sea-changers. I'll welcome them back.

7

Because manners give
us dignity

SOME PEOPLE SEE MANNERS as a veneer, like an overlay of gilt over tin jewelry: strip away the glitter and the cheap true self will be revealed. For some reason, the very people who think this are the ones who most disparage manners—as if we would all prefer to see people at their most base. To me this seems a bleak view of human nature. I see manners more optimistically: the artifice as embellishment rather than disguise. A way to enhance and illuminate the inner self, not to hide it.

Perhaps that's why I find myself dismayed by the comprehensive casualization of modern life. The tradition of wearing your Sunday best was never just about putting on your finest clothes for morning church and Sunday lunch—it was about putting on your finer self, as well. To me an unlit candle is a sad thing—but lit up it serves its proper function and glows.

George Orwell was a progressive man, a thoughtful man, a deeply moral man. He was certainly not one to focus on human trivialities. In his memoir, *Down and Out in Paris and London,* he unflinchingly portrays the indignities of life as an impoverished kitchen hand.

> *We quarrelled over things of inconceivable pettiness. The dustbin, for instance, was an unending source of quarrels—whether it should be put where I wanted it, which was in the cook's way, or where she wanted it, which was between me and the sink. Once she nagged and nagged until at last, in pure spite, I lifted the dustbin up and put it out in the middle of the floor, where she was bound to trip over it.*
>
> *"Now, you cow," I said, "move it yourself."*
>
> *Poor old woman, it was too heavy for her to lift, and she sat down, put her head on the table and burst out crying. And I jeered at her. This is the kind of effect that fatigue has upon one's manners.*

What I find interesting and surprising about this story is the idea that being robbed of one's manners constitutes an assault on one's selfhood as powerful, invasive and disabling as poverty and low status. Manners were important to Orwell: they were a sign of his humanity. And he deeply resented a system that pushed him so hard that he lost them.

To regard manners as a mask that should desirably be cast off is to misunderstand the role they play. When you lose your self-control, when you explode in rage or anger, when you abandon your manners, you are not proudly revealing yourself, you are losing something, some key element of your personhood.

There's a rebuke that's now out of fashion: *Sir, you forget yourself!* It assumes that one's real self is not necessarily the base authentic creature. Rather, the real self is that artificial self, the thoughtful person who subscribes to higher standards of behavior. And it turns out that to be told you have forgotten yourself is actually something of a compliment—it assumes there's something valuable to remember.

❧

In 1528, at the height of the Renaissance, one of the gentlemen at the court of Urbino, Baldesar Castiglione, sat down and wrote a series of dialogues set over four evenings. It was called *The Book of the Courtier*. There's a portrait of Castiglione by Raphael: it reveals a comfortingly open face, with large blue eyes and a soft and melancholy expression.

The Courtier is a curious book. With its almost magical air of courtly idealization, it has been unfavorably compared with Machiavelli's near-contemporary *The Prince*, which unswervingly examines the harsh realities of leadership. And indeed

Castiglione does adopt a more noble view of power: ". . . a man who strives to ensure that his prince is not deceived by anyone, does not listen to flatterers or slanderers or liars, and distinguishes between good and evil, loving the one and detesting the other, aims at the best end of all."

But he had some unique insights into courtly life and the aesthetics of manners. There was one vice above all others that Castiglione thought the courtier should seek to avoid. Affectation. He wrote:

> *Affectation is a vice of which only too many people are guilty, sometimes our Lombards more than others, who, if they have been away from home for a year, on their return immediately start speaking Roman or Spanish or French and God knows what. And all this springs from their over-anxiety to show how much they know; so that they put care and effort into acquiring a detestable vice.*

One can only dream of a society in which the main vice is that people actually try too hard to be learned, to be erudite, to be civilized.

But more than this, Castiglione had a very clear and positive idea of the highest virtue a courtier should aim to possess. He called it, in a lovely Italian word that seems to suggest its own meaning, a certain *sprezzatura*. We have no single English word that does this term justice—it means something like ease and nonchalance and graceful carelessness. Castiglione thought this ease should conceal all artistry and make whatever one says or does seem uncontrived and effortless. He added: ". . . to reveal intense application and skill robs everything of grace."

How lovely, the idea that one might have a high degree of social artistry at all, let alone a desire gracefully to conceal the effort behind it. Though Castiglione was an Italian, his ideas took greatest hold in England, where aristocrats thereafter prided themselves on a certain underplayed and witty persona. When Sir Walter Raleigh spread his cloak over a muddy puddle so that Queen Elizabeth's silk shoes would not get damp—that was *sprezzatura*. Nothing labored or pompous. Just a moment of carefree, joyous, everyday beauty.

And it's true that some people don't just have manners, they have beautiful manners. There aren't many, but if you know such a person, a loving image of them will have already sprung to mind. They are the ones who think of the perfect small gift for the sick friend, or gently draw out the shy stranger, or quietly close the window against the cold draft, or tactfully change the dangerous topic, or subtly reorganize the seating so that the slightly deaf person is able to hear better.

Sadly, I am not one of those people but I know one or two,

and I also know that they vivify life; the prosaic becomes lovely in their hands. I have one friend who graces the world with her manners so lightly, with so much of Castiglione's *sprezzatura*, that I sometimes won't notice at the time but afterward I'll remember and think, *That's right!*

The writer Marcel Proust was famous for his manners. This may surprise those of you who have found it a strain to get through his somewhat inconsiderately long *À la recherche du temps perdu*. But his sensitivity, his delicacy, his refinement were renowned. This was particularly touching because Proust was a lifelong invalid, suffering from allergies, an inability to warm himself and a curious kind of insomnia that meant he could only sleep during daylight hours.

On one occasion, a certain friend of Proust's named Paul Leclercq called to see him at the Grand Hôtel in Cabourg after a hot day's bicycling. The restaurant was full of bare-shouldered ladies and tailcoated gentlemen. But Leclercq was wearing cycling breeches. Proust said to his friend, "Never mind, we'll dine in my room, and I'll serve you myself so that the waiter shan't see you." Sure enough, Proust collected each course from a tray in the lobby of his room, but only when he was absolutely sure the waiter had moved off down the corridor.

Leclercq was touched and amused by this incident. He thought Proust was under the mistaken impression that being seen by a waiter in the wrong clothes would be as embarrassing to Leclercq as it would clearly be to Proust—and decided that this was true courtesy.

But this story has another level. Proust would have been just as concerned for the feelings of the waiters as for his friend. If Leclercq had paraded his wrong clothes, it may have seemed to the waiters like a snub to their dignity and that of their establishment. Proust was probably even more courteous than his friend imagined.

Good manners lend grace to life, but it must be admitted that bad manners can also be enlivening. Of course, they are only really effective when delivered by those with a special gift for it, with an ear for it, like music. They are the ones who know exactly where the line is drawn between consideration and rudeness—and are skillful enough to lift their knee high above that line and land with malicious precision on the other side. One of these was Beau Brummell, the world's first dandy. He took men out of their patterned silks and breeches and dressed them simply and soberly in beautifully cut black suits, adorned with elaborately tied neckwear. He claimed to take five hours to dress, and recommended that boots be polished with champagne. For a long time, he was great chums with the prince regent, but for reasons that aren't perfectly clear, Beau began to lose favor. At this he became vastly annoyed. One night, as the grossly overweight prince strolled past with their mutual acquaintance Alvanley, Beau abandoned his usually impeccable manners and remarked loudly, "Alvanley, who's your fat friend?" In the hands of a beginner, this remark might be vulgar. But it's a delicious zinger coming from the most refined man of his day.

Bad manners may not only be amusing, they may sometimes be the occasion for some of the most beautiful manners of all.

In 2005, the great actress Cate Blanchett was playing the lead in Ibsen's *Hedda Gabler* when something terrible happened to the man in the front row, stage left. His cell phone began ringing. In his hurry to extract and silence the phone, he accidentally flung it onto the stage, where it continued to emit a chirpy ring tone in the middle of late nineteenth-century Norway. At this point an actor calmly walked across the stage, picked up the instrument and handed it to the culprit, who sank back in shame. But taking her bows at the end of the play, Cate leaned forward and patted the culprit on the knee.

Oh, yes, the audience swooned.

. . . improve communication

One of the worst implications of the lack of manners in modern life is that it is now almost impossible to convey subtle messages to other human beings.

Once, we all made efforts to develop what were known as social antennae: to attune ourselves to the ebb and flow of society; to render ourselves capable of responding sensitively to the subtle currents of meaning beneath the noisy river of social discourse. If someone just faintly flicked an eyelid at you, or raised their eyebrows fractionally in your direction, or paused just a little too long before replying to your remark, you would instantly be aware not only that a message was being sent but what that message intended to convey. You knew at once whether it was sympathy or disapproval or warning. More important, others around you would also be aware of this communication, because their social antennae enabled them not only to decode their own interactions, but to interpret the interplay taking place between others, as well.

Someone not long ago castigated me for my interest in manners and complained that I was too soft on the snobbery that inevitably goes hand in snooty glove with manners. I replied indignantly that I was not soft on snobbery, I was *nostalgic* for it. How on earth can someone be a snob in the modern era? Who would notice? We have no dress codes. We have no dining etiquette. We have no rules of conversation. We have no class, in all senses of the word. The sheer brutal enjoyment of snobbery relies upon an accepted in-crowd humiliating an outsider. It only works when everyone agrees there is an in-crowd. And when the outsiders accept they are of inferior status. Maybe I am just moving in the wrong circles, but I am fairly sure an incident that Proust describes in *The Guermantes Way* would be unlikely to occur today. Here are the narrator and the historian being introduced to the duchesse de Guermantes:

> *The historian made a low bow, as I did too, and since he seemed to suppose that some friendly remark ought to follow this salute, his eyes brightened and he was preparing to open his mouth when he was chilled by the demeanour of Mme de Guermantes, who had taken advantage of the independence of her torso to throw it forward with an exaggerated politeness and bring it neatly back to a position of rest without letting face or eyes appear to have noticed that anyone was standing before them; after breathing a little sigh she contented herself with manifesting the nullity of the impression that had been made on her by the sight of the historian and myself by performing certain movements of her nostrils with a precision that testified to the absolute inertia of her unoccupied attention.*

I like to think of myself as reasonably socially alert, but I am fairly sure if someone merely adjusted her torso and flared her nostrils at me, I would be hard-pressed to spot that she was sending me a message about the nullity of my impression.

In modern life it is almost impossible to communicate with people socially. Where once you need only send up a tiny social smoke signal to convey a message about manners, now you have to burn down the whole house.

A friend of mine was once the unhappy hostess at a dinner party where one guest was a bore. Not just any bore, either, but a *home renovation* bore. She tried to distract him, offering more food. She tried to deflect him, turning brightly to another guest, saying, "How is the new job working out, Cecile?" But all to no avail. The offender, absorbed in his own tedious commentary, did not get the message or, more likely, did not care. He continued unconcernedly, unashamedly, to drone on about the rise in the value of his property that was sure to result from the various improvements he was undertaking, despite the assorted sins and failings of his builders, tradesmen, architects, intolerant neighbors and recalcitrant local council.

As the night wore on, my friend's guests began sneaking out one by one, and two by two, casting her either resentful or apologetic glances or both. Of course the dullard remained. My friend got up and cleared the plates. Then she put them in the dishwasher. She stopped filling his glass. Then she took his glass away. She stifled a yawn. Then she didn't stifle a yawn. Then she yawned very loudly. Finally her husband left

the room, brushed his teeth and put on his pajamas. And
when he came back he told the bore that it was time for him
to go home. He refrained from adding: the one you have been
droning on about all evening.

This kind of occasion is very disheartening. It is a strong
disincentive to venturing out in society—or inviting society in.

Of course, society has always had its socially inept members. And I have been one myself, on more occasions than I
care to remember. But it used to be that if someone was becoming tedious at the dinner table, the host or hostess could
deliver a subtle rebuke with little more than a patient sigh and
a delicate wave of the wineglass and the other guests would be
in a position to observe, with sympathy or malice, the ripple
of deflation crossing the blunderer's face as he or she suddenly realized their error and abruptly subsided.

Cruel, yes, but kinder than the modern alternative.
Where once the oblique rebuff or reproof left everyone's dignity more or less intact, now one is forced to deliver or receive
an unambiguous and wounding rejection. Like: *You need to go
home now.*

And on the matter of snobbery, perhaps it is worth noting
that the capacity to use manners wonderfully and well is not
just a matter for the ruling classes. In Gertrude Stein's *Autobi-
ography of Alice B. Toklas,* she describes one of the most subtle

social rebukes I have ever come across. Please note that the spelling and punctuation are all Ms. Stein's.

Hélène was one of those admirable bonnes in other words a maid of all work . . . She was a most excellent cook and she made a very good soufflé. Hélène had her opinions, she did not for instance, like Matisse [author's note: yes, that Matisse]. She said a frenchman should not stay unexpectedly to a meal particularly if he asked the servant beforehand what there was for dinner. She said foreigners had a perfect right to do these things but not a frenchman and Matisse had once done it. So when Miss Stein said to her, Monsieur Matisse is staying for dinner this evening, she would say, in that case I will not make an omelette but fry the eggs. It takes the same number of eggs and the same amount of butter, but it shows less respect, and he will understand.

. . . **prevent premature intimacy**

Let us now imagine a meeting between two acquaintances.
How do you do?
Very well. How do you do?
Very well, thank you.
I trust your family is well?
Quite well. And yours?
Well, yes, it is dull. It is long-winded and impersonal and

artificial. It will take a long time before these two people dis-
close anything personal or private to each other. In fact, if
they proceed as above, they may never find out anything. But
let's be perfectly honest: most people are dull. The slow-
witted will never become more interesting simply because
they are let off the leash and allowed to fully express themselves. This is the one irrefutable piece of evidence amassed by
TV talk programs and reality shows.

Manners offer us the protection of social constraints.
Manners take time, often too much time. But they also confer
time. Time to get to know someone, time to think about how
we feel, time to consider our reactions and respond wisely
and well.

Somewhere there arose the false idea that rapid intimacies
bring people closer together. In fact, all too often they simply
raise the stakes improperly in the early stages of a relationship.
They increase the risks. What if the person from whom you've
taken these intimate details turns out to be someone you don't
really care to know? There you are, burdened too quickly with
their secrets, their private dreams, their hidden stories. The
very artificiality of manners protects us from the temptation to
enter into premature intimacy.

I once had to stop going to a really good hairdresser because I regretted the intimacies that I myself had foolishly
initiated. I realized I had *told him too much*. We'd started kissing

each other hello and goodbye. He talked about having a drink sometime. I just couldn't stand it anymore. If only I'd stuck with a more formal approach. A small artifice can sometimes forestall a large phoniness—or the loss of a great hairdresser.

A friend of mine went on a coffee date with a man she had met at a dinner party. Within five minutes he told her that he had Googled her and discovered she was on the RSVP website—a site that helps people find romantic life partners. Before they had even ordered coffee, he quizzed my friend on whether she wanted children and informed her that he himself had had a vasectomy. This was more information than my friend could cope with at short notice, and she made sure her coffee was an espresso so she could leave in an express fashion, as well.

Every time you read one of those glib lifestyle articles about relationships, it will tell you that the key to a happy relationship is frank and honest communication. This is, on the whole, wrong.

Most of the successful romantic partnerships that I've come across have relied on the considerate withholding of unpalatable truths. A little light deception, you might say, plus a big dash of routine and a great deal of courtesy.

Somerset Maugham once reminisced about the curious marriage between his father and the beautiful woman who was twenty years his junior:

In Paris they were known as beauty and the beast. My mother was very small, with large brown eyes and hair of a rich reddish gold, exquisite features and a lovely skin. She was very much admired. One of her great friends . . . once said to my mother, "You're so beautiful and there are so many people in love with you, why are you faithful to that ugly little man you've married?" And my mother answered: "He never hurts my feelings."

I've seen the forty-plus-year marriage of my own parents held together by fruit-shop flowers every Saturday and a kiss every evening without fail. No matter how much they irritated and even enraged each other, during those inevitable times they did. And they're still together. It's not too much to say that manners got them through their marriage.

People think manners aren't sexy. Transgression is sexy; busting taboos is sexy. How can manners be sexy? But as anyone interested in sex will confirm, deferral is the essence of foreplay. Manners play their delightful role in creating tension, anticipation, curiosity. They respect the essence of each partner's separateness.

Here's beautiful young socialite Millamant being wooed by handsome Mirabell in William Congreve's play of 1700, *The Way of the World*. Millamant is setting up certain strict conditions before she'll consent to marry this young man with whom, by the way, she is desperately in love.

Millamant: *I won't be called names after I'm married; positively I won't be called names.*

Mirabell: *Names!*

Millamant: *Ay, as wife, spouse, my dear, joy, jewel, love, sweetheart, and the rest of that nauseous cant, in which men and their wives are so fulsomely familiar—I shall never bear that—Good Mirabell, don't let us be familiar or fond, nor kiss before folks . . . nor go to Hyde Park together the first Sunday in a new chariot, to provoke eyes and whispers; and then never be seen there together again; as if we were proud of one another the first week, and ashamed of another ever after. Let us never visit together, nor go to a play together, but let us be very strange and well-bred: let us be as strange as if we had been married a great while; and as well-bred as if we had not been married at all.*

To Millamant, the preservation of a certain strange and well-bred distance is not a path to marital estrangement but to lifelong romance. She is fighting for a sexy marriage. And the continuation of a certain distance, far from killing off the relationship, is, in her view, likely to add spice to it. He must always woo her; she will always seduce him.

Congreve's play pokes fun at upper-class manners, but at the core of it all is the way love might be expressed in manners— which hold two people gently apart in order to bind them more closely together.

Those magazines and self-help books that tell you to unload your every little passing thought, feeling and criticism upon your partner are cruelly misleading. When love means never having to say you're sorry, it's nearly always because you weren't unkind to your partner in the first place.

. . . unlock our humanity

The modern conception of great art is that it relies upon tearing down social conventions. But great art, even, and perhaps especially, when it subverts the orthodoxies, relies upon the artist's deep ingrained knowledge of the rules. The greatest artists all started with profound technique, even if like Matisse they ended up making collages of little bits of paper.

The experience of artistry most necessary to me is reading novels. I still remember that my first overwhelming, expanding sensation at discovering fiction was one of relief. That there were people out there who could show me how the world really worked. Who could illuminate the strange and mysterious ways in which adults behaved. Novels, or the great ones anyway, take you outside your own tiny boxed-in perspective and reveal the shades of motive and meaning that guide people in their interactions with each other. Novels make you compassionate, because they show you the deep motivations that drive otherwise indefensible actions.

People have wondered about the rise of nonfiction. But to me it makes perfect sense. Fiction reached its high point in the English language during the repressed Victorian era. It was always a covert way to explore taboo topics—bad marriages, domestic violence, infidelity, larceny, betrayal, treason. But now the taboos have gone. People can—and do—talk openly about the appalling things they have done, or that have happened to them. No topic is off-limits anymore. No subject is too cringe-inducing, humiliating, mortifying or shameful. I was a porn queen, drug fiend, incest survivor, stripper, swinger. I cheated, I stole, I lied, I got away with it, I didn't. We don't need fiction as a way to explore these dirty little secrets anymore. We've got fact.

But this doesn't mean we can do without fiction. The novel is still the art form that most comprehensively grapples with what it means to be human and to struggle along in the world. And many of the greatest novels are comedies—or tragedies—of manners.

Henry James and Marcel Proust and George Eliot and Edith Wharton and Jane Austen and F. Scott Fitzgerald and Anthony Powell are very different authors. But all of them show us people circulating in society: negotiating their way, finding their feet, losing their heads and breaking their hearts.

For me, the greatest pleasures are the revelations of subtle feelings: emotions and sensations that are not normally explored or expressed. When Lydgate in *Middlemarch* slowly shrinks his spiritual aspirations to meet his wife's material ones. When Elizabeth Bennet in *Pride and Prejudice* comes to understand that her beloved father's weaknesses are almost as culpable as her mother's. That terrible moment when Isabel Archer in *The Portrait of a Lady* walks in on her husband and Madam Merle: they are doing nothing more than looking at each other but something in their body language suddenly awakens Isabel to the depths of their complicity. "Society is the stage on which manners are shown; novels are their literature," said Ralph Waldo Emerson.

Sam is a very lovely sixteen-year-old of my acquaintance who likes to watch TV and movies. She also likes to read, but she thinks novels of manners are boring and outdated, preferring fantasy and comedy and action. The problem with each of these genres is that, at their most simple, they are cartoon-like and flattened out. And at their most elevated, they are operatically grand, dealing with heroically inflated figures and black-and-white moral situations. They simply don't deal in the novel's uncomfortable shades of gray.

I once saw Sam's beautiful face ripple with surprise as she experienced a subtle feeling that she could not name, and for which Homer Simpson's *Doh!* and *Woo-hoo!* or even the grand moral dilemmas facing the hobbits in *Lord of the Rings* offered no satisfactory explanation. Because it was just a simple human experience: the first time she had been socially bested by a skilled hypochondriac. As the conversation proceeded, I could see Sam beginning to realize that no degree of sympathy or boosting would suffice; that offering her limited experience of ill health was not welcome; that the hypochondriac's manipulative self-pity and narcissism were inexhaustible. Sam could do no right. If only Sam had made Mr. Woodhouse's acquaintance in Jane Austen's *Emma*, she might have been better equipped to cope—or at least to recognize simply that here was a familiar human type, and that she was part of a long and honorable continuum of hapless victims.

The phony sitcom half-feelings of *Friends* or *Seinfeld* don't lessen our capacity for real feelings, but equally, they do not enhance our capacity to understand them. When we eliminate literature from our lives, we deny ourselves the wisdom of generations of authors who reveal not only the surface of human nature but what lies beneath. The inner selves that are so hard to find and touch and understand.

The path to those inner selves is always through the outer world. Manners provide not just the formal structure but also the prism through which we can engage with the deepest things.

. . . and make life beautiful

I recently read that a series of ballroom dancing films had stimulated certain schools to teach children how to dance. The aim was to use dance as a vehicle for inculcating civility. Of course. Dance teaches manners. When we hold each other in our hands. When we support and strengthen each other. When we learn to trust. In dance we embrace the separate unity, the distinct wholeness, when two people move as one. And the outward structure provided by dancing is an aid to inward development.

There's an extraordinary moment in the best of all Fred and Ginger films, *Swing Time*. The lovers have met the insurmountable hurdle in their romance. It's over, it's insoluble, they can never be together, although they must, for they are truly in love. Fred sings to Ginger that without her he'll never dance again. "Never gonna dance," he warbles in his thin true voice, "Never gonna dance, only gonna love, never gonna dance . . ." Now, in their evening clothes, they walk across the dance floor. They are close but not touching. Their heads are lowered. They are beautiful and sober and sad as they grieve for the fact that they'll never dance together again. When suddenly you realize that their walking—their non-dancing—has, imperceptibly, turned into dancing. Their last dance.

As Fred and Ginger glide and turn, they pay homage to

their own love story, repeating snatches of dance sequences from other scenes in the movie, as if their whole relationship could be summed up in his swoop and her dip, his lean forward and her lean back, his weight and her flexion, as indeed it could.

Can there be a better metaphor for civilization than two dancers twirling in joyous and respectful synchronicity?

AFTERWORD

Looking back over all I have written, I appear to have made some outlandishly extravagant claims for manners. Such as, for example, healing the planet, inoculating us from a police state, restoring our citizenship, saving our marriages and making our lives richer and filled with meaning. Hmmm.

Perhaps I'll end on a smaller note.

Most Saturday mornings at 9:15 I can be found in a large old hall with long wooden floorboards and high rafters on open black beams where, with a small class of regulars led by our teacher, Sana, I do yoga.

Sana is about twenty-eight years old. When, lying on her stomach, she raises herself up on her hands and rolls her chin and eyes upward in cobra pose, she looks distractingly like a supplicant Renaissance Madonna—if that Madonna had worn a T-shirt and sweatpants.

The ritual is always the same. Breathe in, breathe out. In, out. In. Out. Downward dog. Plank. Child's pose. Head up. Scoop to cobra. Breathe in. Breathe out. Up again to plank. Back to downward dog. Breathe. Now it's standing poses. Triangle pose. Warrior One. Spear pose. Mountain pose. Hold. Hold. Breathe. Relax.

Of course, the practice of yoga is physically and spiritually beneficial. And then there is the curious diversion of looking at the world via the triangle between your legs. The back of a hall gains a certain interest when viewed upside down. The dust floating on a sunbeam seems still more delicate from under your armpit. You become aware of ancient cobwebs on the ceiling as you lie on your back holding your knees to your chest. And as you lean your body forward and twist your torso to the back of the room, you notice with sleepy affection the unbrushed patches of your classmates' Saturday morning heads.

After years of yoga together, we students know very little about one another's professional qualifications, income, career highlights, domestic arrangements or belief systems—these matters never arise. Instead we know the important things: whose knee is tender, whose back is weak, whose hamstrings are tight. You get to know another body very quickly when you're pushing a hip or twisting a shoulder or compressing the outer ankles to the floor during partner exercises.

In yoga, sometimes the body takes over—a surprised fart makes its way to the surface, or a snore rolls up to the rafters and expands across the hall. Once, a man began weeping, hard and painfully, and the atmosphere became suddenly very still, as if the class were collectively bearing witness to his distress.

Often at yoga all you can hear, no, all you can feel, is your breath rising in and out in your flesh. And where your body seems, usually, so weak and heavy, as you lunge and lift yourself and pull the air in and push it out and dimly hear the matching sounds around you, you suddenly feel that all human life is as powerful as this—this in and out and in and out. And as frail.

Toward the end of the class we all lie quietly on our mats, and Sana will take us through a relaxation exercise. I rarely comply with her verbal guidance, and instead of emptying my mind or letting thoughts disappear like passing clouds, I let the words and sentences gather and frame in my head.

In its unassuming way, this weekly ritual reminds me what manners require, and can achieve. The way it balances the needs of each individual and the demands of the group. The poise it creates between self-discipline and relaxation, submission and assertion, privacy and intimacy, order and freedom. The sense of private integrity in a communal space.

Manners do matter. Because, by our individual contributions, our little, petty sacrifices, we dignify ourselves. And we combine to make something bigger than ourselves. A civil society.

FURTHER READING

Aristotle. *Nicomachean Ethics*, translated by Terence Irwin, Hackett, Indianapolis, 1999.

Clive Bell. *Civilization: An Essay*, Penguin, London, 1928.

Edmund Burke, *Reflections on the Revolution in France*, Yale University Press, New Haven, Connecticut, and London, 2003.

Baldesar Castiglione, *The Book of the Courtier*, translated by George Bull, Penguin, London, 1967.

Lord Chesterfield, *Letters Written to His Natural Son on Manners and Morals*, Peter Pauper Press, Mount Vernon, New York, 1936.

Collected Works of Erasmus, Volume 3, University of Toronto Press, 1985.

H.D.F. Kitto, *The Greeks*, Penguin, London, 1951.

Harold Nicolson, *Good Behaviour: Being a Study of Certain Types of Civility*, Constable and Co. Ltd, London, 1955.

Robert Sutton, *The No Asshole Rule: Building a Civilized Workplace and Surviving One That Isn't*, Sphere, London, 2007.

Alexis de Tocqueville, *Democracy in America and Two Essays on America*, translated by Gerald Bevan, Penguin Classics, London, 2003.

ACKNOWLEDGMENTS

I am grateful to Jane Palfreyman, who suggested I address the subject of manners, and to Tim Whiting in Australia and Amy Einhorn in the United States for their support and advice. Special thanks to my editor, Nadine Davidoff, for her support and professionalism. A fellowship at Varuna, The Writers House, gave me invaluable time and space. My writers' group: Vicki Hastrich, Eileen Naseby and Charlotte Wood, has been essential both to joy and writing. Many dear friends helped me greatly with their editorial advice, kind support, book loans and tales of manners. Gratitude deserves individual thanks, but courtesy to readers demands brevity—so I shall simply say thank you all very much. A loving thank-you to the Holdforth family. And to Syd Hickman, who makes it all possible.

ABOUT THE AUTHOR

Lucinda Holdforth lives in Sydney and is a speech-writer. Her first book, *True Pleasures: A Memoir of Women in Paris*, was published in 2004.